Teen Mom Confidential

Secrets & Scandals From MTV's Most Controversial Shows

By Sean Daly & Ashley Majeski

Think you know everything about **Amber Portwood**, **Jenelle Evans**, **Kailyn Lowry**, **Maci Bookout**, **Farrah Abraham**, **Catelynn Lowell**, **Chelsea Houska**, **Leah Messer** and the rest of MTV's famous young moms?

Think again! From how the girls of 16 and Pregnant were cast to the *Teen Mom* stars' outrageous diva demands and the touching letter from **Stormie Clark** to the granddaughter Farrah won't let her see, these are the true, behind-the-scenes stories of TV's most fascinating and controversial shows.

Forget the rumors. *Teen Mom Confidential* is packed with first hand memories, newly published photos and updated interview with the cast members everyone is talking about.

"Teen Mom Confidential"

By Sean Daly & Ashley Majeski

Roundup Publishing, Santa Monica, CA

For more information, contact Editor@TeenMomConfidential.com

First printing: April, 2013

Printed in The United States of America

ISBN: 1481004077
ISBN-13: 978-1481004077

ACKNOWLEDGMENTS

The authors wish to thank **Farrah Abraham, Daniel Alvarez, Butch Baltierra, Jamie Blackwell, Cleondra Carter, Stormie Clark, Tyler Cooksey, Casey Cunningham, Danielle Cunningham, Ashley Danielson, Nicole Fokos, Hope Harbert, John Hidalgo, Jordan Howard, Andrew Lewis, Kailyn Lowry, Amy LaDawn Nichols, Ebony Jackson-Rendon, Jamie McKay, Alethea Montante, Sarah Roberts, Gary Shirley, Josh Smith, Katie Stack, Sabrina Solares, Dawn Spears, Robert Thompson, Toni Ziegler** and the many other family, crew and cast members who agreed to be interviewed for this book.

CONTENTS

Introduction

MY STRANGE ADDICTION

By Ashley Majeski

My name is **Ashley** and I am a reality TV junkie. I'm the first to admit I have a strange life: I spend my nights on the couch watching cheesy "unscripted" shows and my days blogging about them for *TheAshleysRealityRoundup.com.* Never could I have imagined how much of my website – and my life – would be taken up by MTV's controversial docu-series *16 and Pregnant* and *Teen Mom.*

For the past three years I have been learning everything I can about **Amber Portwood**, **Maci Bookout**, **Catelynn Lowell**, **Jenelle Evans**, **Chelsea Houska**, **Kailyn Lowry**, **Farrah Abraham**, **Leah Messer** and the rest of basic cable's most notorious young mothers. Writing about this bunch can be a full time job. There are arrests, weddings, divorces, daddy dramas...

In just the first few weeks of 2013:

- Leah had a baby.
- Jenelle suffered a miscarriage, dumped husband **Courtland Rogers** (after just 53 days!) and filed assault charges against him.
- Kail revealed she was pregnant again and suffers from bipolar disorder.
- Farrah was arrested for D.U.I. – and blasted on social media for waxing her three year-old daughter's unibrow.

- Catelynn and fiancé **Tyler Baltierra** began filming episodes of an upcoming reality series called *Couples Therapy* – just months before their planned wedding.

As you can see, it's tough to keep up! Luckily, I have help. Back in 2011, I met **Sean Daly**, a reporter for the *New York Post.* He needed some information for a story about the new season of *16 and Pregnant.* I had never thought of myself as any kind of authority on the subject, but then it hit me. Perhaps after years of documenting these girls' dramatic journeys from small town obscurity to the front page of *TMZ*, I had in fact become an expert on the new MTV: "Maternity Television."

Sean and I ended up working together on several projects and eventually decided to collaborate on this book. Our goal was to tell the complete – and uncensored – stories of these shows and their stars: the good, the bad and what got left on the cutting room floor. We spent a full year reaching out to everyone we could find who had ever been associated with the productions: crew, family members and especially the girls themselves. We dug up shocking details MTV never wanted anyone to see – like how some important events (including one *Teen Mom 2* girl's scandalous hookup) were completely staged or recreated.

MTV basically invented the genre of reality television back in 1992 with *The Real World.* But these shows have been groundbreaking in a completely different way. Not too many years ago – (before **Bristol Palin** and **Jamie Lynn Spears**) – girls who got pregnant in high school were sent to "visit their aunt in the country" to prevent bringing shame on their families. Now they're welcomed into our living rooms as unwitting role models – baby bellies in full view — to share their polarizing stories of what happens when you get knocked up before you can vote.

Each year, almost 370,000 American teens incur an unplanned pregnancy. Only a dozen or so make it to MTV. This is the true story of those girls, and how three shows changed their lives — and reality television - forever.

The Great Debate:

Does MTV Glamorize Pregnancy?

"The message that I take from the shows is that it's cool to become pregnant... Being a teenage mother is making them famous."

- LaToya Hagins, *Examiner.com*

"Anyone who has seen even one episode of either of these shows can see that these girls' lives have been completely turned upside-down by their pregnancies. Most struggle just to keep their baby's father in the picture on top of trying to finish high school and scraping together enough money to feed, clothe, and otherwise care for a newborn."

- Melanie Boysaw, *Berkeley Political Review*

"I had an abortion when I was 16. Because that's what I should have done. Otherwise I would now have a 20-year-old kid. Anyway, those are the things that people shouldn't be dishonest about. *16 and Pregnant*? Getting rewarded for being pregnant when you're a teenager? Are you serious? I mean, that makes me want to kill somebody."

- Chelsea Handler, talk show host

"I'm so tired of hearing that *Teen Mom* glamorizes teen pregnancy. I've been on my own and a single parent since I was 17. Is that glamorous? I don't have relationships with either of my parents and I struggle dealing with teenage emotions and adult responsibilities. That's glamorous?"

- Kailyn Lowry, *Teen Mom 2*, via Twitter

Chapter 1

MEET THE TEEN MOMS

They began as ordinary high school girls – cheerleaders, athletes, future college students – and ended up as the most famous moms in America. With nearly seven percent of all girls between 15 and 19 becoming pregnant in 2008, MTV casting directors had no shortage of underage baby bumpers to choose from for their groundbreaking new docu-series, *16 and Pregnant.*

Season one premiered to over two million viewers on June 11, 2009 and featured just six one-hour episodes. Each storyline was more gripping than the next: unsupportive families, the painful choice to give up a child for adoption, the tragic death of a loved one. These stories are "ones you treat with kid gloves," former executive producer **Liz Gateley** told the *New York Post.* "There are moments that you have to turn the cameras off and you have to comfort them."

Ultimately, four of the girls – **Farrah Abraham**, **Maci Bookout**, **Amber Portwood** and **Catelynn Lowell** – were selected to continue documenting their journeys on the spinoff, *Teen Mom*, in 2009.

AMBER PORTWOOD

(b. May 14, 1990)

The hot-tempered Hoosier had been dating **Gary Shirley** for more than two years when she became pregnant with daughter **Leah** (b. November 12, 2008). They planned to marry, but the relationship quickly turned violent. During season one of *Teen Mom*, Amber was caught on camera trying to choke Gary after he insulted her father. Weeks later, cameras rolled again as she punched and kicked him in front of their daughter. Amber was charged with two felony counts of domestic battery and spent one night in jail. Gary was eventually granted custody of Leah as Amber's personal and legal woes mounted.

FARRAH ABRAHAM

(b. May 31, 1991)

Life for the aspiring model and actress from Council Bluffs, Iowa changed overnight when boyfriend **Derek Underwood** was killed in a December 2008 car wreck. Derek, Farrah has maintained, was the first and only love of her life – though she revealed in a 2012 autobiography that he was unaware he was the father of her daughter **Sophia** (b. February 23, 2009). Despite his paternity, Farrah refused to allow Derek's family to see the baby for years, prompting a lawsuit from his mother. In January 2010, things also got complicated at home, when Farrah's own mother, **Debra Danielson**, was charged with assaulting her. "That was, like, the lowest point with my family," Farrah revealed during a *Teen Mom* after show interview.

CATELYNN LOWELL

(b. March 12, 1992)

The high school senior from Algonac, Michigan – and her boyfriend **Tyler Baltierra** – struggled for months with their decision to give daughter **Carolynn "Carly" Elizabeth** (b. May 18, 2009) up for adoption. The couple paid tribute to their baby by each getting tattoos bearing her name. Catelynn and Tyler have been together since the seventh grade and plan to marry on their ninth anniversary on July 15, 2013 – even though he is already her stepbrother. (Tyler's father **Darl "Butch" Baltierra**, a mullet-sporting, recovering drug addict who is in and out of jail, married Catelynn's mother **April** after their kids started dating). Just 16 when she became pregnant, Catelynn told *MTV.com* she understood what birth control was, but never knew how to get it and was afraid of everyone knowing she was sexually active.

MACI BOOKOUT

(b. August 10, 1991)

A popular, outgoing softball player, Maci had dreams of going away to college and becoming a broadcast journalist. Then she got pregnant. Suddenly, she was enrolled in courses at the local community college – and struggling to take care of newborn son **Bentley** (b. October 27, 2008) without much help from baby daddy **Ryan Edwards**. The couple lived together briefly and even considered marriage, but their tumultuous relationship eventually imploded. The fight over custody and visitation with Bentley became even more strained when Maci began dating former childhood pal **Kyle King**, who is four years her senior.

Teen Mom 2, which premiered January 11, 2011, introduced a new crop of girls with even more legal woes and daddy dramas:

LEAH MESSER

(b. April 24, 1992)

Once a popular cheerleader, country girl Leah is now the mother of twin girls **Aliannah** and **Aleeah** (b. December 16, 2009). A graduate of Herbert Hoover High School near Charleston, West Virginia, Leah got pregnant on prom night – the first time she had sex with her boyfriend of one month, **Corey Simms**. She went into labor three months early and was forced to remain on bed rest for the duration of her pregnancy. Leah married Corey on October 17, 2010 but they divorced six months later after he learned that she cheated on him just a week before their wedding. With one of her girls suffering from a mystery ailment that slowed her development, Leah continued working part-time as a dental assistant while taking online courses at Mountain University. She eventually began dating pipe-liner **Jeremy Calvert**. They married on April 4, 2012 – just months after Leah suffered a heartbreaking miscarriage. Her second marriage is "different from Corey and my relationship," Leah told *Us Weekly*. "Because we were kinda like forcing it... With Jeremy, you know when you're supposed to be with somebody and you're not."

JENELLE EVANS

(b. December 19, 1991)

The ultimate bad girl from Oak Island, North Carolina has a growing rap sheet and a volatile relationship with her mother, **Barbara**. No longer in contact with baby daddy **Charles Andrew Lewis**, she drinks, smokes pot, steals credit cards and isn't afraid to open up a can of whoop ass on anyone who crosses her. When Jenelle couldn't curb her excessive partying, Barbara stepped in to take temporary custody of son **Jace** (b. August 2, 2009).

KAILYN LOWRY

(b. March 14, 1992)

A former high school lacrosse player from Nazareth, Pennsylvania, Kailyn wanted to give her baby what she never had: a loving, two parent family. She worked two jobs to support son **Isaac** (b. January 18, 2010), while tackling a full course load at Northampton Community College. Early on, "Kail" said she tried to hide the pregnancy from friends at school. When her mother **Suzi** – who struggles with addiction – moved into a motel with her boyfriend, leaving Kailyn essentially homeless, the teen who dreamed of becoming a dental hygienist took up residence at baby daddy **Jo Rivera**'s house. Unfortunately, they fought all the time and he wanted nothing to do with her – until she started dating someone else. Kailyn's dad, **Ray**, took off when she was just six months old. He now lives in Texas in a home with no back door, but a lock on the freezer – to protect his $200 stash of meat! She saw him again for the first time during her episode of *16 and Pregnant*, but hasn't had contact with him since.

CHELSEA HOUSKA

(b. August 29, 1991)

A star softball player in Vermillion, South Dakota, Chelsea's dreams of attending beauty school were put on hold when she went into labor five weeks early with daughter **Aubree Skye** (b. September 7, 2009) on the first day of her senior year. The youngest of four daughters, she received lots of support from her family – especially dad, **Randy**, a dentist – but almost none from boyfriend **Adam Lind**. Chelsea tries every option to make their relationship work, despite Adam's constant claims that she is "nagging" and "annoying." But when he goes M.I.A for three weeks after Aubree's birth – and sends Chelsea an abusive text message calling their daughter "a mistake" – she decides to cut the cord and promptly changes Aubree's last name to her own.

RIPPED FROM THE HEADLINES: JANUARY 29, 2013

Teen Mom 2 Cancelled: Is Jenelle To Blame?

According to the *New York Post*, the decision to end the show followed several months of erratic, headline-grabbing behavior by the loose cannon star. In that time, Jenelle became pregnant (again), got married, lost her baby and publicly demanded a divorce. She also posted what appeared to be disturbing play-by-play updates of her seven week pregnancy ending on Twitter. "And this is the end, I think," she shared with 632,800 followers. "Feel light headed." Hours later, Jenelle tweeted that she was with her ex-fiancé, Gary Head, at a North Carolina bar. Insiders said producers were concerned the attention-seeking reality star had become too much of a liability for the show.

SEC

The Girls - At A Glance

LOCATION

Of the 47 baby mamas featured during the first four seasons of MTV's *16 and Pregnant....*

28 (59%) are from the south (south of West Virginia and east of Texas)

9 (19%) are from the mid-west
6 (13%) are from the north
4 (9%) are from the west

Texas claimed the most participants (**8**), followed by Florida and Pennsylvania (**4** each).

2 girls were from Riverview, Florida: (**Markai Durham** and **Jennifer Del Rio**)

EDUCATION

31 (66%) Graduated high school

6 (13%) Earned a G.E.D.

4 (9%) Dropped out

6 (13%) Still enrolled

22 girls were at one time enrolled in college or trade school

RELATIONSHIPS

9 (26%) married their baby daddies

5 (56%) of those marriages ended in divorce

15 (32%) are currently together with the fathers of their babies.

BABIES

49 babies have been born

25 (51%) were girls

24 (49%) were boys

There have been **2** sets of twins

The most common baby names are Ayden and Noah, with two girls naming their babies each of those names (although they are spelled differently)

3 (9%) have chosen adoption.

LEGAL TROUBLES

12 (25%) have been arrested

3 (6%) have served time in jail

3 (6%) have lost custody of their children

"I don't know why we are not picketing out MTV. These are the kind of shows that are so disgusting with what they are promoting and they are pretending that they are showing how horrible teen pregnancy is? I call bullshit on that! You are not doing anything but making girls want to be pregnant. Now they are big celebrities. They get endorsement deals. They are on television. They have no right to be on television. They have done nothing to be on television."

- LEAH REMINI,
ACTRESS

Chapter 2

16 AND PREGNANT...AND FAMOUS

Amber Portwood was drifting in and out of consciousness. She lay face up on the living room sofa – a rope around her neck, according to some reports – when police and paramedics arrived at her Anderson, Indiana home on June 14, 2011. The high school dropout was still reeling after losing custody of her two year-old daughter, **Leah**. Now convinced that her baby daddy, **Gary Shirley**, was cheating, she consumed what friends believed to be a potentially lethal combination of pills. Amber, who had privately been under a psychiatrist's care for almost two years, was "distraught," police reports say, "and threatening to end her life."

Amber's desperate cry for help came just one week after she pled guilty to domestic violence charges for beating the bejesus out of her on-again-off-again boyfriend during a blowup at their apartment. The jaw-dropping attack had been captured by MTV cameras and eventually turned over to Child Protective Services. Now with mounting legal problems, a crumbling home life, and her most intimate struggles playing out in front of four million viewers each week on TV, the girl who once dreamed of opening her own beauty salon had finally hit rock bottom.

At a time in their lives when most girls are consumed with *Facebook*, school work and finding a prom date, Amber and the 46 other mostly lower income girls featured on *16 and Pregnant* and *Teen Mom* were doing their best to navigate the perilous waters of parenthood – while still growing up themselves.

Like Amber, many of the girls quickly became overnight tabloid celebrities – their faces and personal stories splashed on magazine covers and entertainment news shows around the world. "MTV can be as objective as they want about it, but once these young women are being followed by tabloids and on *TMZ* and on the cover of *Us Weekly*, it's hard to view them as documentary subjects," **Jessica Coen**, editor of *Jezebel.com,* told *ABC News.* "They're reality stars."

The night that Leah's episode of *16 and Pregnant* aired, her producer phoned with an ominous warning: "Your life is about to change forever." "Leah had no idea what she was getting herself into," her former best friend **Amy LaDawn Nichols** tells us. "She never thought she'd ever be on a magazine cover or involved with paparazzi or anything."

MTV, a network unafraid to push the boundaries of taste and exploitation, billed its most controversial series yet as "cautionary tales" about the perils of young motherhood. "What people connect to in these stories and on this show is family," former executive producer **Liz Gateley** told the *New York Post.* "Everyone can relate to family and what buttons get pushed in a stressful situation. That is why, I feel, people are tuning in to these shows."

16 and Pregnant, the brainchild of MTV development executive **Lauren Dolgen**, was filmed in a no-frills, documentary style. Each episode took viewers inside the homes, schools and workplaces of its struggling, young subjects as they coped with money problems, cheating boyfriends and unsupportive parents.

"Awkwardly crunching pregnancy, childbirth and the first few months of parenting into an hour, the documentary-style program eschews tough questions and works too hard at entertaining, turning a potential public service into a bit of a muddle," *Variety* television critic **Brian Lowry** wrote of the premiere episode, which featured fresh-faced high school cheerleader, **Maci Bookout**. "Even her 30 hours of labor is dispatched in a few seconds of pencil animation, making the act of childbirth look about as difficult as an a-ha video."

Still, the girls' lives and journeys, in no small way, became symbolic of middle class life in the era of Obama. Scratch the surface of these emotional sagas and everything you need to know about America comes flowing out.

"In my experience, freshman and sophomore girls want babies," says cast member **Jamie McKay**, who was featured on *16 and Pregnant* during season three. "They watch the show out of envy, when really it's showing them what they don't want."

When it comes to creating dramatic and polarizing TV, you won't find much better material than a young girl who clearly doesn't have her own life together suddenly ending up responsible for a tiny, hungry, pooping, screaming human being. Or, says **Robert Thompson**, a pop culture expert at Syracuse University: "Pregnancy itself is about as dramatic as it gets. Placing that onto a teenage girl – especially the ones that they choose – how could you not be compelled to watch this?"

Naturally, MTV has tried extra hard to convince people the shows are essentially public service announcements – kind of like the movies about car crashes they show you in high school to discourage drinking and driving. But critics – and there are lots of them – say paparazzi shots of girls shopping, partying and spending their *Teen Mom* paychecks on boob jobs send the opposite message and are actually encouraging some impressionable teens to get knocked up.

"There are...kids now who think it is cool now to be a teen mom," notes actress and reality star **Tamara Mowry**. "[They think] 'They are on covers of magazines. They're famous... so why don't I have a baby? If they can do it, I can do it.'"

At one point in 2011, **Chelsea Houska**'s housemate **Megan Nelson** was pregnant – at the same time as three of **Jenelle**'s best friends. Though **Keely Sanders**, **Amber Painter** and **Lauren Pruitt** all supposedly lectured Jenelle about becoming a teen mom at first, their loyal and trusted pal **Kristina Collins** told *In Touch* magazine: "I think all the girls idolized Jenelle. Lauren has even mentioned how cool it would be if she got her own spin-off show."

Megan, who became an unwed mother herself in July 2011, claimed that her pregnancy was a complete surprise. But her friends were quick to call bullshit on that. "[Megan] purposely got pregnant in order to become a regular on the show," one squealed to the tabloid. An MTV spokesperson later told the *New York Post* "none of the friends of the girls on the show have reached out to producers to get their own shows or get on [TV]."

Whitney Purvis – one of the teens featured on season one of *16 and Pregnant* – may need some extra convincing of that. In fact, she's stated that she, too, sometimes meets people who "are wanting to get pregnant just to be on the show." Whitney hasn't given any interviews since getting arrested in March 2012 for stealing a pregnancy test from Walmart (and using it in the store's bathroom!) but she did talk to *ABC News* not long after her episode aired. "I meet people who are changing their life just for what I did," she said. Then the big bombshell: "There's actually two girls who got pregnant just for that and they went to the same school and MTV had to wind up picking either one of them...so they picked one of them and then the other one, you know, is just sitting there!"

Whitney – like other girls featured on *16 and Pregnant* – was compensated $5,000 for her appearance, which MTV reserves the right to show an unlimited number of times anywhere in the world.

Details about financial compensation have been shrouded in mystery for years. Confidentiality agreements forbid most participants from discussing how much they get paid. While there have been many reports that *Teen Mom* cast members earn a cool $65,000 per season, our sources – including several of the girls themselves – say it is actually much less.

Here's what else we know:

Who gets paid and who doesn't?

For *16 and Pregnant*, only the female stars and their baby's father are compensated. (As part of her deal, each girl is also required to appear on the "Life After Labor" finale special. MTV pays for travel.) For the *Teen Mom* shows, only recurring cast members – boyfriends, mothers, husbands, etc. that appear for multiple episodes – take home a check. According to one show insider, the baby-daddies (along with **Jenelle's** mother, **Barbara**) make the same amount for each episode they are in. If they do not appear, they do not get paid.

Our sources say most secondary cast members (which includes friends, family members and boyfriends) get paid about $2,000 a season. And everyone appearing on camera is required to sign non-disclosure agreements. Compensation for secondary personalities is completely negotiable. Some friends and family members have stopped filming, or refused to participate altogether, in order to secure better deals. **Jeremy Calvert**, the man that eventually married *Teen Mom 2* star **Leah Messer**, hated dealing with the camera crew and didn't want to be on the show. So producers had to offer him a lot more money than usual to appear.

It's simple economics, really. The more intricate someone is to the storyline, the more they will get paid. **Gary Head**, who was Jenelle's boyfriend during the fourth season of *Teen Mom 2* was paid only $1,500 for appearing on several episodes, while **Kieffer Delp** negotiated for significantly more. Another perk: the network will pick up the bill whenever the main subject and her friends or family are filmed dining out – ("But only up to $20 per person," one cast member says) – or if they are participating in an outing set up by the show for filming purposes.

"Most of our friends hate filming," one insider says. "MTV sets all of those scenes up with our friends so in turn they have to pay them to film, almost like a bribe."

Do all the *Teen Mom* girls make the same amount?

Sources say the girls from all three *Teen Mom* franchises each earned a base salary of $10,000 in their first season. They were guaranteed pay bumps to at least $25,000 in season two. During a court proceeding in December 2010, Amber revealed that she took home $140,000 for six months of work, but it does not appear that came exclusively in the form of a paycheck. "We definitely don't make nearly as much as most websites and magazines say we do," one of the girls insists. "It isn't even enough to pay one month of my bills."

Do the girls get paid when stories about them appear in magazines?

Sometimes. Recurring cast members (friends and family) are forbidden to talk to the press without approval from MTV. Many of the articles that appear in supermarket tabloids are actually placed by the network for promotional purposes, and thus, there is no exchange of money. To supplement their income, some girls have sold stories or photos to the media through a friend or relative. Leah and Jeremy reportedly picked up around $10,000 for selling her wedding photos (without the consent on MTV) to *Us Weekly* in 2012.

Do the girls get bonuses?

Yes. Cash bonuses are sometimes awarded for high ratings – but most girls say they are rare. More often they receive items such as restaurant gift cards.

Does MTV buy the girls houses and cars to keep them on the show?

No. All of our sources tell us that these rumors are completely false, and that MTV has never made any big-ticket purchases. But several of the *Teen Mom* girls have used their TV money to splurge. Other things that are never covered by producers: any sort of grooming services, such as manicures, hair styling, plastic surgery or tanning. The girls pay for those things on their own.

Do the babies make any money from appearing on the show?

Yes. The babies on all of the *Teen Mom* shows (except *16 and Pregnant*) each have trust funds set up by MTV, which they can access when they turn 18.

What does MTV pay for when the show's stars have to travel for show-related work?

Insiders say the show will reimburse its stars up to $75 a day for food and expenses when they are required to travel for show-related work. Their hotel expenses and airfare are also covered, as are the travel costs for some family members or friends that will appear on the reunion shows, or come to help babysit the star's child while they are working.

Does the show provide medical insurance and benefits to the cast?

No. The girls are not considered employees, and therefore are not given the benefits you would get at a regular job, such as medical insurance or a 401(k) plan. Each cast member receives a 1099 form and is responsible for paying her own taxes at the end of the year, as no money is withheld from their checks. On occasion, this has caused the stars of the show to run into trouble with the IRS. In March 2013, **Kail Lowry** revealed on *Twitter* that she had to cancel her upcoming wedding reception because she owed thousands of dollars in taxes.

Gary's 9-1-1 Call

Gary Shirley sensed something wasn't quite right after a frightening conversation with Amber Portwood on the morning of June 14, 2011. At 11:34 AM, he called 9-1-1 in Anderson, Indiana looking for help.

Operator: *Anderson 9-1-1, what is your emergency?*

Gary: *Hi. I just spoke with my, uh, girlfriend and she had said something to me... She is Amber Portwood...Um, she said something to me...said she's having a hard time in her life. (She said) 'Call the police, they will find my body in the garage.' I don't know what to do. So I am calling you guys because I don't want her to kill herself... This is about 5 minutes ago. I called my mom...she was like "She has made several, she has said this several times" and I said "She is not answering my phone calls. She said 'call the police so they can find my body in the garage.' I called her back several times and she didn't answer, so... You don't tell somebody to call the police if you don't want them to call the police.*

Operator: *Is she home by herself?*

Gary: *Yes, she is. I called my mom. She is on her way over there right now.*

Operator: *What kind of car is she going to be in?*

Gary: *She's not in a car. She'll be in the garage, and in the garage she has Dodge Magnum in her...she has a Dodge Magnum in her driveway.*

Operator: *Wait a minute. You said your mother's going over to check on her?*

Gary: *Yeah, but I don't...*

Operator: *And she'll be on foot?*

Gary: *She's going to hang herself!*

IN CASE OF EMERGENCY
Call 911

Chapter 3

WHERE DO THEY FIND THESE PEOPLE?

Sharon Bookout was combing through Craigslist ads in the spring of 2008, hoping to find a modeling job for her pregnant teenage daughter, **Maci**. What she stumbled onto instead was a casting notice for a new cable docu-series that planned to follow teens like hers on their scary and unpredictable journeys into unplanned parenthood:

> *MTV is currently casting an upcoming series focusing on young women during their pregnancy. As we realize that this is a sensitive subject that many of our young women are experiencing, our goal is to show what pregnant women, from varying backgrounds, are experiencing in their everyday lives.*
>
> *From morning sickness to mood swings, and to even the day of the baby's arrival, we would like you to let us document this exciting, life changing event. Similar to the MTV series* True Life *or* Engaged

> & Underage, *our show will allow these young women to share their story in their own voice.*
>
> *As time is of the essence, please email me ASAP at [redacted]. Please include what state you are in, your contact details, a picture and why you would want to take part in the series.*

Maci, a popular, athletic cheerleader at Ooltewah High School in Chattanooga, Tennessee, was immediately interested. But Sharon remained skeptical. "[She] thought that it was a fake," the young mom revealed during a speaking engagement at the University of Central Florida in 2011. "So she had my dad come with me to make sure I wouldn't be kidnapped!" The ad, of course, was legit. And *16 and Pregnant* soon became the first show to shine a bright light on a topic that had long been too taboo for television.

For creator **Lauren Dolgen** a key part of the show's success was the decision to keep the producers' opinions out of the final product. "It's completely from the point of view of the girls who are going through it," she told *Slate.com*. But before any stories could be told, producers had to find the right girls, so casting notices were plastered all over pregnancy message boards, MySpace, and anywhere else teen girls might gather online. The search was on for a compelling group of real-life "Junos."

"The goal was to try to find a typical, middle-class teenager who should have known better," executive producer **Morgan J. Freeman** told the *Los Angeles Times* in 2010. "The mandate was 'get the truth. Let's see the real challenges, what pressures it puts on high schoolers, what the sacrifices are.'"

One of the first girls cast was **Ebony Jackson** of Colorado Springs, Colorado. Just 17 and already engaged, she came to the attention of producers through The Pregnancy Center, a local Christian organization that helps pregnant teens once they decide to keep, and parent, their babies. Ebony was in the first semester of her senior year at Mitchell High School and, though she was pregnant, was determined to remain in the Junior Reserve Officer Training Corps. Her hope was to join the military after the baby was born.

Ebony was completely unaware of the nationwide casting call. So was **Cleondra Carter** – one of 12 girls featured in season three. "I never watched the show after the first season because it just annoyed me to be honest," she says. "They only showed the downfall of being a teen mom and stuff that a baby can 'take away,' when none of that is true." Cleondra, just 17 and uninsured when she became pregnant, was actually contacted directly by casting scouts after being referred by a local health center near her home in rural Mississippi.

"This woman named Claudia told them about me because she thought I had a good head on my shoulders," she remembers. "The next thing I know I have voicemails on my phone from MTV asking if I would be interested. After I found out that I was pregnant, it probably took them like two to three weeks to contact me."

Amber came to the attention of casting scouts almost by accident. They were hoping to recruit her brother **Shawn** (and his now ex-wife, **Samantha Hall**) for a show called *Engaged & Underage*, which followed young couples as they prepared to say, "I do." "I told them that we were already married and they said, 'that's fine,'" Shawn revealed on his personal blog. "They wanted to do a special with us. [MTV wanted us to] get married and then turn around and tell our families that we had been married for over four months at the time. I told them that they were not going to make a mockery out of my life."

Months later, another casting director reached out to Hall, asking if she knew anyone who might fit the bill for an upcoming show about teenage pregnancy. She suggested 17-year-old Amber, who was newly pregnant by Shawn's former friend, **Gary**.

Amber's long, storied history with MTV began – as all the girls' did – with a simple questionnaire. "Then you have to film a day in the life of yourself and include your family and your boyfriend/girlfriend," season three's **Danielle Cunningham** explains. "If you make it that far and they're still interested in you then they send out a test shooter and see how you act on camera. [There are] quite a few steps, like five...You have to take a personality test, meet with a counselor who makes sure you're not crazy. There is a background check and then you meet with producers after you are chosen."

"I knew it would ruin her life. I wish Amber would have had the same mentality as me [and turned MTV down]."

- SHAWN PORTWOOD

Shawn – who had been away on deployment to Iraq while the casting process played out in his home – was furious with Amber for going through the entire process and agreeing to participate on the new show. "I knew it would ruin her life," he wrote. "I wish Amber would have had the same mentality as me [and turned MTV down.]" But she didn't.

Neither did 16 year-old **Whitney Purvis**, who was living in tight quarters with her grandmother, and mother – who was also pregnant – in Rome, Georgia when she was cast. Purvis said films like *Juno* made pregnancy look "cute" and wanted to show the unfiltered reality of being irresponsible in the bedroom. "You know you don't have to have sex," she told *ABC News*. "(But) if you do, be smart because this is what happens."

Producers – eager to explore what happens when girls decide to give their babies up for adoption – also reached out to Bethany Christian

Services, a faith-based adoption agency in Grand Rapids, Michigan. There, they discovered **Catelynn,** a 16-year-old from nearby Algonac, who was considering placing her baby up for adoption. Catelynn submitted the mandatory audition video, much to the shock of **Brandon** and **Theresa Davis** – the North Carolina couple that she (and boyfriend **Tyler**, 16) had already selected to adopt their baby. Though initially nervous to be a part of the series, the couple eventually agreed to allow the adoption process to be filmed.

Chapter 4

MAKING TV MAGIC:
TALES FROM BEHIND THE SCENES

Kailyn Lowry was fuming as she watched the second season finale of *Teen Mom 2*. The most quiet and conservative of the show's four young mothers says she was ready to quit when producers edited footage to make it appear that she and ex-boyfriend **Jo Rivera** had hooked up for a soap-filled romp in the shower!

"MTV wasn't there [when Jo and I hooked up] but they tried to play it like they were," Kail tells us. "They had us reenact it. The scene where I tell Jordan about cheating on him was reenacted. That's why I was so coldhearted. Jordan already knew about it at that time, and we had already moved past it, but they made us reenact it and live through it again, and then again when it aired. It really upset Jordan. We had broken up and had gotten back together. Jordan had no choice but to do it because he was under contract, too. There was a point that I wanted to quit and rip up my contract because of the way they treated me."

Like many of the MTV girls, Kail agreed to share her very personal story because she was sold on the "documentary" style of series. Her day-to-day interactions – and the struggle of raising son **Isaac** on her own – would be portrayed to viewers exactly as they unfolded, she believed. Wrong! What the heavily tattooed 20 year-old didn't realize was that both *16 and Pregnant* and the *Teen Mom* franchises are carefully crafted by a team of directors, editors and producers, who ultimately shape each girl's on-screen persona and decide how their individual stories will play out on TV.

"They just beefed it up with drama," says **Sabrina Solares**, who appeared on the fourth season of *16 and Pregnant*. "I don't want to show my daughter Audrey [the episode]. I just wish they showed [the good stuff] rather than the drama."

Danielle Cunningham, a fan favorite from season three says producers would purposely instigate conflict during the filming process, in hopes of capturing dramatic blowups with boyfriend, **Jamie Alderman**, on camera. "They would tell us to talk about touchy subjects that would cause us to fight," the Ohio teen tells us.

Whitney Purvis, one of six girls featured during season one, told a similar story to *ABC News* in 2009. "They would take you in separate rooms and then they would film me with my friends and my boyfriend with his friends and just get you to talk about the things you don't like about each other," she said. "They want you to argue. They want you to talk about each other. They want you to get where you want to break up with each other to go stay at separate places. I just didn't like that at all."

Neither did season three's **Cleondra Carter,** who claims footage in her installment of *16 and Pregnant* was purposely pieced together to make her boyfriend, **Mario Escovedo**, "look like an asshole." Of course, she concedes, "during some of the filming it was him who was making himself look like an asshole!"

The filming process was "emotional and exhausting" says **Katie Stack**, one of three teens featured in the 2010 special "No Easy Decision," which featured *16 and Pregnant* season two's **Markai Durham** as she contemplated having an abortion. "The actual staff and crew of MTV were amazingly supportive," Stack tells us. "They really went above and beyond to make sure that we felt supported through the process – even coming to our hometowns to let us see the show before it aired, so we could be prepared. I've maintained relationships with many of them."

Still, Cleondra says, nothing was off limits once cameras started rolling. "They made us film EVERYTHING!" she says. "You could never get out of it. I remember when I did not want them to film when Mario and I were at Sekesui [a restaurant in Memphis] and we got into that argument." While MTV team members never put exact words in her mouth, she says "they would just get things out of us that we would seriously never have talked about. They were like counselors with cameras."

Other girls say the often eight-member production crew was more like paparazzi. Danielle, just 16 when she became pregnant with son **Jamie** during junior year, says it was an ongoing struggle to shield her friends and family from overly-invasive cameras during personal, private moments. "[My ex-boyfriend Jamie's] dad got evicted and I refused to let them film it," she says. Danielle also contends MTV crews tried to get a little too up-close-and-personal while shadowing her in the fall of 2010. "I refused to let them film me pumping milk," she remembers. "I felt that it was an invasion of privacy. They actually begged me to let them film it.

They were very forceful. They would say things like, 'This is your story so let us film what's really going on!'"

Capturing each girl's story is a full time job that usually begins around the fourth or fifth month of pregnancy. Each girl is assigned a director, producer and camera crew to trail her up to 13 hours a day for approximately one week each month. "It's one of the worst jobs I've had," one former camera operator posted during a bombshell August 2012 Q&A chat on *Reddit.com*. "Opticalsk" – whose identity we have agreed not to disclose – also revealed several other interesting tidbits about what goes on behind the scenes:

*** Members of the production staff must remain completely removed from the action – even in situations where babies could be in harm's way.**

"As a camera operator i'm not allowed to interfere. legally can't even hold the babys. the producer/director's would interfere and shape the 'story'." [sic]

*** Conditions inside the girls' homes are often dirty and disgusting.**

"Every shoot i would want to call CPS. filthy houses (dog poop on the floor, bloody tampons sitting in a corner for months, weeks old food everywhere, etc) one of the worst is Leah (Messer), filthiest person i've met. when feeding her twins she would spill a bunch of cheese puffs on the nasty carpet and the girls would crawl around and suck up the cheese puffs, no hands involved. this made me cry a few times."

*** The production company has a policy in place for when abuse or neglect is suspected – but nobody follows it.**

"[The] rule was to file your complaint with production manager. if the production manager felt that they were legally bound to submit the

complaint to the authorities they would. of course they never did. it took a lot of alcohol to fall asleep. i couldn't take it half way through the 3rd season and quit." [sic]

*** Some members of the film crew would try to party with pals of the girls they were filming.**

*"One crew member was caught in the hot tub at our hotel with one of the girls friends. He was promptly fired. She asked for his age. He was 38. She started screaming and *beep* hit the fan. He is bald and always wears a cap. Looks young with the cap. In the tub he took it off. She was like WTF!"*

"It gets to the point where the director is feeding them lines."

- FORMER *TEEN MOM* CAMERAMAN

The veteran cameraman also confirmed multiple reports that episodes of both shows are "heavily scripted." "It gets to the point where the director is feeding them lines," he said. In some cases, entire scenes are set-up and inserted to speed up or fill in blanks during the story telling process. "They recreated key things like walking up and down stairs, in and out of doors," says **Jamie McKay**, who shared her experience of welcoming daughter **Miah** during season three of *16 and Pregnant*. "They made [my boyfriend] Ryan go back to the hospital and recreate going inside."

"One part in my episode where [Mario] was in a red hoodie and he was throwing the ball back and forth with the dog was SO FAKE!" Cleondra adds. "I understand their concept of how it was already hard to get him over to my house, but that was just crucial. I had no idea about it and I was mad as hell when Mario told me. After they finished that scene, he walked over to my house and was like 'Don't be mad, they told me to say that.' I was like 'Wow!'"

It turns out Cleondra's episode wasn't the only one with re-enacted or completely fabricated content. In the summer of 2011, 23 year-old **Daniel Alvarez**, a recent college graduate from Austin, Texas, briefly dated new mom Farrah after she relocated to Florida. Their six-week courtship was documented and shown over the course of several episodes during the final season of *Teen Mom*. "The day they filmed me 'meeting' [Farrah's daughter] **Sophia**, I had to pretend like I had just met her, even though I had already met her and hung out with her," he confesses. "They needed to get it on film. They also made us do things like say we were on our second date and pretend we were just meeting again even though we had been dating for awhile already..."

Alvarez, who provides marketing and brand recognition services for a company in Austin, says producers staged numerous other events, including his introduction to Farrah's mother, a horseback riding date ("I didn't really want to go because I don't like horseback riding, but they wanted to get us dating on film") and a July 4th fireworks outing. ("It was weird with the people from the show there. They would make us do things over and over again so they could get the shot they needed.")

Still, there were some moments producers only got one crack at. In each episode of *16 and Pregnant*, the money shot was the birth of each child. Film crews would hunker down at a nearby hotel beginning two weeks before the projected due date and the girls were under strict orders to call their main producer the moment they went into labor. "[The crew] had just left my house probably like four to five days before," Cleondra remembers. "I was blowing up my director, Allison's phone. I went into labor at 1 in the morning and she probably did not answer until around 5 AM. They got on the plane after that. As soon as she made it to the hospital, [my daughter] **Kylee** was coming. After she came in the room to say 'hey,' I began to push."

As Cleondra recalls, the MTV crew "had the hardest time getting clearance" to film at the hospital. "They never got it, actually," she admits. Instead the episode's director had to pretend to be a family member to gain access to the delivery room. Producers ran into the same problem in season two with Florida teen **Nicole Fokos**. "They had to sneak little Flip cameras in there," Nicole remembers. "They got caught with that, too. [The hospital] started threatening everybody that they were going to call security. My mom was like 'This is her cousin. He's just filming it.' But they didn't believe it."

Most of the show's participants have remained quiet about their experiences – until now – because of intimidating confidentiality agreements they are required to sign with producers and the network. MTV has been notorious for the way it has exploited reality show contestants for more than two decades. In 2011, the *Village Voice* dropped a bombshell on the former music channel by exposing the 25 page agreement signed by each house member featured on another reality show, *The Real World*. Among the stipulations:

* *You may be humiliated and intentionally portrayed "in a false light."*

* *Producers can make any changes they want to your life story.*

* *Camera crews can show up to your home at any time to film and may take anything they want -- as long as it gets returned once production has ended.*

Terms for the participants on *16 and Pregnant* and *Teen Mom* – which are produced by 11th Street Productions, but still in close conjunction with MTV – are equally restrictive. Several of the girls tell us they are forbidden to make drastic changes to their personal appearance, including hair color and style. On occasions where a "new look" cannot be worked into the show, some girls have been forced to wear wigs and hats.

"If they need to film a pick up, which is when they weren't there for certain things and they need to go back in time [and restage what happened] sometimes they have to get creative to make it look like no time has passed," one insider says.

Producers reportedly panicked when **Jenelle** (following the lead of **Maci** and **Farrah**) decided to get a boob job in the summer of 2012.

In Her Own Words:
Jamie McKay

Did the producers ever try to get you to talk about certain things?
They never told me what to say, just what to talk about. They just wanted me to help catch people up. But there were times I didn't want to talk about certain things, like when Ryan showed up with a hickey on his neck to Miah's birth. I didn't want to talk about that at all and they made me.

Were you allowed to stop them from filming if something was happening that you didn't want shown on TV?
They said they wouldn't put whatever we didn't want [shown] in. But during the "Where Are They Now" special I told them not to show the part where my mom and I are arguing [but they still did.]

How many MTV crewmembers were in the room with you at the hospital while you were giving birth? Did the hospital give them any problems?
One, and they weren't allowed in until I said it was OK. Before the epidural I was feeling really bad. [The hospital didn't give us] any trouble, but I was told I was one of the last births they got to film.

Possibly sensing the backlash the show would receive if all of its "struggling" young stars were able to afford pricey cosmetic procedures, producers sent the word out that plastic surgery was strictly off-limits until after the series ended.

The biggest – and most problematic – stipulation for many of the girls: social media postings are strictly monitored and no one is permitted to talk to the media without an MTV representative present or on the phone. Anyone who violates the gag order is subject to a fine of up to $1 million, several girls have said.

But that hasn't stopped some former cast and crewmembers from opening up about their experiences participating on the show. "We get in trouble all the time for what we post on *Twitter*," one cast member says. Predictably, 18 year-old **Megan McConnell** received an immediate order to remove the following 2011 post from her personal blog, which details how she say producers bullied her into reading "a bunch of lies" during the narration for her episode of *16 and Pregnant*:

As most of you may know, I was on MTV's hit series 16 and Pregnant. I was part of season 2-B. I like to consider our season as the "forgotten step child" because most people don't remember the season. Being on TV was a cool, once in a lifetime experience. Unfortunately, once the show aired I had no desire for it to ever play again.

They depicted my family and I completely wrong, and the worst part? My voice overs were pretty much all lies! I would say 90% of the stuff they MADE me say was a lie. It took 5 hours to record voice overs because I fought every little bit of it. All they would say was "We can't change it now because everything is already timed with the episode." That made sense to me, but they should have run it by me before making everything official.

One of the things I had to lie about was my dad being active duty. He has been retired from the Army ever since I was 10 or 11 years old.

He does still work over seas, but as a security contractor. He now works for a very important, and top secret company. Another thing I had to say was "I've never been outside of our tiny town". That is a complete lie. Think about it, a military family, never moving, living an hour and a half away from the closest Army base. Yeah, right. Those were the two main ones that bothered me.

A week before we flew out to film the reunion, Nathan and I had a big fight and broke up. He ended up not coming with me to New York. That p!ssed off MTV so they completely redid my entire show, to make him look horrible. Sure, he did say some mean things, but he didn't intend for them to come out that way. When he said something like, "If it weren't for the baby, I wouldn't be here" he meant that if I wouldn't have gotten pregnant he would have moved to Texas with his friend in search of work (which was brought up later in the show). Yes, he was still immature and partied, but not nearly as often as they made it seem.

Oh! The part where I was at the Halloween Party and it showed me texting Nathan, that was also a lie. I was either texting my mom or checking my Facebook *because I was bored, I didn't text him at all the night. One way I know they made it up, I spell everything out when texting and I don't use the term "wtf". He was at home that whole night, and I knew he wasn't coming to the party. He told me days before that he was going to hang out at home and I was fine with it.*

When they came out to film the catch up show, we knew that we had to watch what we said because they're good at twisting our words. We were much happier with that segment.

Needless to say, I will NEVER work with MTV again.

In Her Own Words:

Danielle Cunningham

What was your filming schedule like?
They came at like 8 AM and we would film everywhere the director said we needed to. They would leave at like 10 p.m. They came like once a month, and then like three times a month around the end of filming. They would film for about 13 hours a day.

Did you have to call the producers when it was time for the birth and other major events?
Yes, we would call them. If they couldn't fly straight down from New York fast enough, we would film ourselves with a Flip cam. For labor, they stay in a hotel nearby for the two weeks before you're due so they can rush right over when it's time.

What was the downside of exposing your life like this? Do you regret doing the show?
The downside was for sure the negative feedback I get from people. I hate that everyone in the world knows my personal business. I can't even have a *Twitter* and tweet what I want to tweet because so many people judge.... I try not to regret anything but [I] kind of [do regret it.] But I would still do it all over again, just differently."

What didn't we see on TV that happened during this time?
A lot! A lot of drama, crying, fights...plus I worked full time while 9 months pregnant. They didn't show any of that which pissed me the hell off.

What were the best and worst parts of your experience?
The best part was that it was basically the chance of a lifetime. I mean, I've been asked for my autograph, how freaking sweet is that? I also gained a new family. I miss my camera crew. The worst parts were that they controlled my life way too much. It was ALL about MTV. They scratched the hardwood floor my dad had just put down with their equipment and didn't care. One time I was in pre-term labor but they wouldn't let my mom take me to the hospital until they got the car lighting just right. It was bullshit!

SE(

Chapter 5

BEFORE THEY WERE TEEN MOMS

Before she became a notorious reality TV star, **Farrah Abraham** was a lot "like **Lindsay Lohan** in *Mean Girls*," her half-sister, **Ashley Danielson** remembers. "Popular, but not mean or cruel." A Barbizon model and boy-crazy cheerleader at Thomas Jefferson High School in Council Bluffs, Iowa, she was "very quiet and reserved," says former best friend and classmate **Tyler Cooksey**. "Nothing like you see now."

Farrah and her sister were raised in an upper-middle class, two-parent household – unlike many of the other MTV moms. "We went on a lot of big family vacations - road trips, Disneyland, etc.," Ashley tells us. "We had a lot of fun growing up and were very blessed. We always had our family supporting us in the audience at school plays, recitals, contests, science fairs, etc." But Farrah's childhood story is no fairy tale.

Her mother, **Debra Danielson**, met future husband **Michael Abraham** in 1987. Debra – just 31 at the time – was fresh off of a divorce and struggling to raise six month-old Ashley on her own. Debra, who worked in software sales, and Michael, a manager for AT&T, hit it off and married about a year-and-a-half later. And so began a long, often strange relationship, that even today, Ashley admits she doesn't really understand.

"I think we both knew their relationship was a wreck and they are two people that really had no business getting married to each other in the first place," she says. "My mom was a good mom when we were growing up. She wasn't perfect but she tried." Debra ran a tight ship at home. Farrah and her sister were kept on a rigid schedule of extracurricular activities that included dance classes, piano lessons, and various sports. The girls were also given strict curfews, expected to complete a list of chores – and taught the value of a dollar from an early age. At 15, Farrah began her first non-modeling job in the bakery of the local Hy-Vee grocery store. "We have both always been hard-working and had jobs, sometimes two at a time, as soon as we could," Ashley says.

That work ethic, Tyler believes, could be one reason for Farrah's sometimes icy demeanor on television. "Her parents raised her differently than most people are used to," he says. "Money is a big thing to the Abrahams. They don't see each other as 'Mom and Dad' or 'daughter' all the time; they see each other as beneficiaries and business partners."

For years, Farrah privately struggled with identity and self esteem issues. "I remember that I always felt like I wasn't loved enough," she confessed in a 2012 memoir. "[My parents] were always working, or out of town, or fighting. I remember always having to be patient, to wait my turn for their attention, but it seemed like it was never my turn."

Ashley says she remained "very close" with Farrah – "until the point when she met [boyfriend **Derek Underwood**]."

A young Farrah Abraham poses in front of the Christmas tree with mom, Debra and dad, Michael.

Their relationship, she insists, "was toxic. I didn't meet him for a long time, close to a year I think. And I didn't see Farrah that entire time either. Derek [who eventually became the father of Farrah's daughter, **Sophia**] was controlling, to say the least. So when people say Farrah treated Derek poorly, I tell them no. It was most definitely the other way around."

Daniel Alvarez, who became close to Farrah when they dated in the summer of 2011, says Farrah often talked about her relationship with Derek, often sharing shocking details of their fights.

"They had a terrible relationship from what she told me," he says. "The stuff she would tell me about their relationship was insane. Very high drama. They had a lot of fights, cheating back and forth. They hated each other and then loved each other. It wasn't normal. It was to another level and was a very bad situation from what she told me."

Tyler, who also knew Derek well, remembers their relationship differently. "[Farrah] treated him a lot like she treated her parents," he says. "She was a little disrespectful at times to him. Sometimes rude. He would ignore it and pretend she wasn't doing that, just like her parents do."

Debra and Michael discouraged their daughter's relationship with Derek, right up until he was tragically killed in a December 2008 car wreck. Though they were often dealing with their own relationship problems – a cycle of breakups and make-ups that lasted for years – they wanted Farrah to focus on school.

Debra, a deeply religious woman, was also concerned about who her girls were hopping into bed with. "It was beat into my head – wait until marriage," Ashley says. "Be careful who you pick as a husband/boyfriend. The Bible says premarital sex is a sin, etc." Unfortunately, Farrah didn't get the message. She and Derek were sleeping together just one month into the relationship. Their first time was at Farrah's house on the night of Derek's junior prom. "When we woke up a few hours later, my first thought was that I wasn't a virgin anymore," she wrote in her 2012 memoir. "I felt like I now had a huge secret to keep. I was relieved [that my parents] weren't more suspicious...I was convinced anyone could read my face and know that I had had sex."

Meanwhile, Tyler says that when she wasn't with Derek, he and Farrah were partying – right under Debra's nose! Farrah would frequently head to all night teen drinking parties, or sneak her boyfriend into their house for a late-night romp.

"Debra was kind of possessive," he remembers. "She wanted to keep Farrah as sheltered as possible. [Michael] is laid-back, cool, collected, and rarely got angry. But when he got angry, it was bad. As kids we were really mischievous. We loved to push people's buttons. She would talk back to him or deliberately not do what he asked."

In her book, Farrah recounts the night in 2008 when Michael flew into a fit of rage and struck Derek after walking in on them having sex.

As part of her punishment, Farrah was promptly shipped off to her grandparents' house for three weeks.

Not long after, Farrah confided to Tyler at cheer camp that she had missed her period. "We were very...social, if you know what I mean," he says. "Getting pregnant was always a risk but we didn't want to think about it." When a trip to Planned Parenthood confirmed Farrah's worst suspicions, Tyler says he broke down in tears. "It changed my life. Life became completely different. We acted more mature. We dressed more grown-up. All the partying stopped. Before, we would drink, smoke, and do anything bad that we could."

Farrah kept the news from her parents until she could no longer hide her baby bump. "They were pretty pissed off, to put it lightly!" Ashley remembers. "But they soon got over it and accepted it." Despite her pregnancy, Farrah continued modeling, working and going to school. She even managed to keep her place on the cheerleading squad.

Farrah kept her decision to appear on MTV secret from even her closest friends. "She never told me she was doing it," Tyler says. "One day I went over to her house to hang out and there were cameras following me. For the next nine months of my life I wore a microphone and had cameras on me at all times. They were in my house. They were at school. They were everywhere, and I wasn't even pregnant!"

At school, he remembers, "People kept asking Farrah if she was on the news or something!" But by then, the rumor had begun to circulate that Farrah was pregnant. When the cameras arrived, it added more fuel to the rumor's fire, says Tyler. Once Farrah confirmed that she was, indeed, pregnant, things got too hard for her at school. In December 2008, she left high school and went to a local college to finish up her high school degree. During this time, she was also dodging Derek's constant calls. He was desperate to know if the rumors that she was pregnant with his baby were true.

Two months before she gave birth to her daughter Sophia, on December 28, 2008, Derek was tragically killed in a car accident. Just after 1:00 AM, Derek lost control of his car, wrapping it around a utility pole and killing himself and his friend, **Zachary Mendoza**. Although alcohol was later determined not to be the cause of the crash, Zach's grief-stricken mother, Jackie, was still arrested in May 2009, after it was discovered that she had purchased a bottle of Skyy vodka for the boys just hours before the crash.

Farrah begged producers to keep Derek's death out of her episode of *16 and Pregnant*, and even told them she was not attending his wake (although she ended up making a brief appearance). Debra, meanwhile, was looking for other ways to make the best of Farrah's situation. Two weeks before Sophia's birth, she insisted they host a baby shower for underprivileged moms-to-be. MTV cameras filmed the event, held at a homeless shelter in Omaha, but it was never broadcast.

REPORT: AMBER TRIED TO HANG HERSELF!

Amber's early years were marred by bouts of depression, cutting and pill popping – mostly brought on by her hot-tempered father's battle with booze.

"When she was 15, before she met Gary, Amber was in such psychological pain from the turmoil in her family that she tried to hang herself from the shower curtain rod in her bathroom," biographer **Rozzie Franco** told *The National Enquirer* in 2011. "She actually wrapped a towel around her neck and tied it to the curtain rod, but it would not hold her weight."

In a bombshell interview with Franco – for a book about Amber's life that never ended up getting published – the troubled star called her father **Shawn** "an alcoholic" and admitted he was "verbally abusive" during her childhood in Anderson, Indiana. **Samantha Hall**, Amber's former sister-in-law shared a similar story that year with

HollywoodLife.com: "Amber's dad treated (her) mom the same way Amber treats Gary – like, 'Shut up bitch!"

The Portwood clan – at times too poor to afford basic telephone service – planted roots in Anderson (pop. 56,125) long before Amber became the area's most notorious resident. Her grandfather **Frank**, an Army veteran, owned several local businesses including the popular Art's Varsity Pizza. Shawn left town briefly in the mid-1980s and headed to Florida, where he met then 20 year-old **Tonya Webb**. They married in Orlando on May 3, 1987, and soon after, their first child, **Shawn Jr.** was born in Atlanta. When Amber arrived on May 14, 1990, the family decided to head back to Indiana. But, sadly, their troubles and struggles continued.

On December 20, 1995, when Amber was just five, Tonya gave birth to the couple's third child, a daughter named **Candace**. Less than a month later, the baby tragically died from Sudden Infant Death Syndrome (SIDS). Amber has admitted she never quite got over the loss. "I remember it like I just watched a movie yesterday," she revealed

Amber Portwood with mom, Tonya, dad, Shawn, and brother, Shawn, Jr.

during the *Teen Mom* season three reunion special. "I remember a stretcher coming in. I remember my mom screaming. I remember her on the edge of the bed. I remember my dad's reaction."

Tonya, too, has haunting memories of her family's saddest night. She had just gotten off work and returned home, where her husband was looking after the kids. After checking on the newborn, she instantly knew something was seriously wrong. "I picked her up and just realized that she wasn't breathing," the still-grieving mom revealed to **Dr. Drew Pinsky** as MTV cameras rolled. "She hemorrhaged from the nose. Immediately, I just checked out."

In the months that followed, Tonya struggled to lift herself out of depression, while Amber put on a brave face for her young classmates at Greenbriar Elementary School. The little girl, who loved Barbie dolls and wearing dresses, made friends easily, childhood friends say. "Amber has always had a fun-loving personality and so many friends she always stuck up for and was always loyal to," one told *RadarOnline* in 2010. "She talked to everyone and never thought she was better than anyone else." But that soon changed.

By the time she enrolled at North Side Middle School, Amber had become aggressive and frequently acted out. At 13, she started experimenting with drugs. "We would always have pills around," Amber told Franco. "Everybody could get pills from everywhere. We would ditch school, stay around the house and take pills. It was my way of escaping and not thinking about my real life."

With their father in and out of the hospital for liver problems related to alcohol abuse – [he eventually developed cirrhosis] – both Amber and her brother began regular sessions with a therapist. In 2005, Tonya had an extramarital affair and decided to finally leave the family home, according to Franco. Shawn joined the Army and headed to basic training, while Amber, just 15, began dating Gary, one of his best friends. Despite their age difference – he is four years her senior – Amber finally believed she had found true love. They dated for two and a half years (and often neglected to practice safe sex) until the inevitable happened: Amber got pregnant. At the time, Shawn was deployed in Iraq and didn't find out until months later that his sister was not only pregnant, but had also decided to share her story on MTV.

"It wasn't really a big shock when I found out I was pregnant," Amber told Anderson's *Herald Bulletin* in 2009, adding that she had always believed she would marry Gary and have his children. In fact, Amber seemed completely unfazed to have a baby on board, telling the newspaper, "It was just the perfect situation. It just happened a little sooner than we expected."

At 18, Amber was the oldest girl chosen to appear during season one of *16 and Pregnant*. She may also have been the saddest. "She told me, 'I was stuck in a dead-end situation at school with no desire to study, a dying father and a mother who chose her boyfriend over me,'" Franco said. MTV cameras captured her dropping out of Anderson High School but made no mention of the fact that Amber had recently been diagnosed with bipolar disorder. (She would later also be diagnosed with dissociative disorder, which caused her to "black out.") producers left out many of the details of Amber's early life and her father's struggle with alcohol. (Her mother also had problems with booze, causing her to be arrested on Christmas Eve, 2007 for driving while intoxicated.)

On the day she was sentenced to five years in prison for her crimes, Amber told the judge she wished she had never agreed to do the show.

MACI WAS A CHEERLEADER, SOFTBALL STAR

Maci Deshane Bookout is a second-generation teen mother. Her older brother Matthew was born just weeks after mom, **Sharon Galbraith**, graduated from Hixon High School near Chattanooga, Tennessee. Against tremendous odds, Sharon – who married Maci's dad, **Billy "Gene" Bookout** that same year – managed to juggle two kids and college, eventually earning a Bachelor's degree. She quickly became Maci's biggest inspiration.

"I think Maci, in her mind, thought that she could do it, because we did," Sharon revealed during the *Teen Mom* Farewell Special in 2012. The Bookout kids, just three years apart in age, were both popular with their classmates and involved in various sports. Maci was a cheerleader in middle school, rode dirt bikes and competed in beauty pageants. But softball was her true passion. She continued to play right up until becoming pregnant at age 16.

By the time MTV cameras set up shop at the family's Tennessee home in September 2008, Maci was already well into her eighth month of pregnancy. "At first, it was extremely awkward having people constantly hanging around the house," she told students during a 2012 speaking engagement at Slippery Rock University. "In the beginning, I didn't understand what the big deal was because I'm just Maci. I never thought I was that interesting."

Audiences disagreed. Her episode of *16 and Pregnant* – and future installments of *Teen Mom* – were chock full of drama between the pretty strawberry blonde and her always complaining ex-boyfriend, **Ryan Edwards**. One of the most popular guys at Ooltewah High School, Maci considered Ryan to be quite a catch and many of her classmate were green with envy. "Ryan...was THAT guy in high school," classmate **Melissa Powell** wrote on her personal blog. "He was absolutely beautiful, I remember that clearly. I'm pretty sure he drove a huge, lifted truck. He played football. He was friends with the 'popular' people. Maybe he was the popular one."

Like most girls at O.H.S., Maci was infatuated with Ryan from the start. "He was so cute, and I just wanted to look at him all the time," she confessed to the Slippery Rock students. "He had a really pretty truck and, you know...the things that are just so important in your partner when you're 16."

It took Maci just three short months to be overcome with passion and move their relationship into the bedroom. “I was the one who talked him into having sex with me,” she said. “Apparently, since I was a virgin, he was scared of me. I thought there was something wrong with me. But, you know, I finally talked him into it.”

What Maci forgot to talk about was birth control, and soon she began her journey into unplanned parenthood. “If you think of how cool it’s going to be that I get to get married, and move out and have a family...[I] just look at the bright side,” Maci revealed in the casting tape she filmed for *16 and Pregnant* in 2008.

Unfortunately, Ryan, wasn’t exactly ready to settle down so quickly. “Back then, I felt like it was just another relationship, nothing really serious,” Ryan revealed during the 2012 Farewell Special.

Two months had already passed by the time Maci discovered she was pregnant. She had taken a test after throwing up while taking a shower one morning, and it had come back positive. After telling her brother, Matt, Maci then had to decide how to break the news to her mother. She finally decided to tell her in a text message. “I stared at that text message for about 15 minutes before finally hitting send!” she revealed during a 2011 speaking engagement. Sharon and Gene were devastated. “That was the first time I had ever seen my dad cry,” Maci said during the *Teen Mom* Farewell Special. “The day I told him I was pregnant.”

Despite apparent strains in their relationship early on, Maci became engaged to Ryan on her 17th birthday. They often talked on camera about tying the knot, although both later revealed that they never believed the wedding would actually take place.

CATELYNN CARED FOR HER ALCOHOLIC MOTHER

Catelynn Lowell, age 3

"Catelynn had a tough childhood, but we did the best we could," her grandmother, **Judith Mitti** told *Star* magazine in 2010. "There was some disfunctionality. I'm not gonna say that there wasn't. But [her mother] had a rough way to go." Growing up in Marine City, Michigan – 63 miles from Detroit – Catelynn would often assume the role of parent, nursing her booze-loving mom after long nights at the bar. "I would put pillows underneath her head while she was passed out on the table," the wise-beyond-her-years teen told *RadarOnline* in 2012. "I pretty much saw my mom drunk almost every day. I had to grow up really fast."

The oldest of three children, Catelynn was born to 19-year-old **April Lee Stotts** and 22-year-old **David Lowell** on March 12, 1992. David, an auto plant factory worker, began pursuing April when she was just 17 and still in high school. She soon dropped out and the couple moved in together. Within a year, April had followed in Judith's footsteps and become a mom at age 19. As the young couple struggled to make ends meet, April's battle with the bottle began to tear them apart. According to her current husband, **Darl "Butch" Baltierra**, April started drinking regularly at age 14.

"Catelynn had a good life when she was a little girl and April and I were still together," David insisted in an October 2010 interview with *Star* magazine. "But there was a lot of partying going on back then, and when I reached a point where I'd had enough, April wasn't ready to stop."

David said he'd had enough by 1994, and packed his bags when Catelynn was just two years old. "There'd be drunks all over our house, and I was afraid for our daughter," he said. "I tried to get custody of her but it's near impossible for a father to get custody in Michigan." So he moved to Florida, remarried and had more children, while April continued to struggle with her addiction. April and Catelynn moved frequently, and during her early years, Catelynn lived in several different states, including Ohio and Texas.

As Catelynn began grade school, April became pregnant again with her second daughter, **Sarah**. (She later had a son, **Nicholas**, with a third man.) Despite their distance, David says he never forgot about his little girl. In 2001, he took April to court, claiming that she was neglecting their daughter, but the court dismissed his claim. Six years later, he arranged for Catelynn to move in with his parents. Her grandmother, Deborah, assumed the role of legal guardian.

Catelynn thrived in Florida but she eventually moved back to Michigan to be with her mother and attend middle school. Enter **Tyler Baltierra**: another troubled teen from a broken home, whom she first met in seventh grade music class. Almost instantly, the pair became inseparable. "I have loved her since the moment I saw her," Tyler wrote on his website. "Her punk rocker hair and attitude matched perfectly for my edgy, hyper personality. I asked her why she fell in love with me and [she told me, and] I quote 'you could always make me laugh.'"

Catelynn with mom, April, and sister, Sarah, circa 2004.

They've been together ever since – except for a few short breakups – and maintained their relationship even after Tyler failed the ninth grade and had to transfer to an alternative high school. In 2008, Catelynn introduced Butch to her mother. A year later, they married and the teens became step-siblings. Despite their unique family dynamic, Catelynn and Tyler remained inseparable. So it was no surprise when Catelynn became pregnant during her junior year at Algonac High School.

Today, the couple continue to defend their decision to place their daughter, **Carly**, up for adoption. "We were so young, and we didn't have anything. I didn't have a job, a car or any money to raise a baby. I didn't have the things a child needs and deserves," Catelynn told Bethany Christian Service's *Lifeline* magazine in 2012. "And I didn't have mental stability. I was so young. I definitely wanted Carly to be raised in a Christian family. I wanted her to be in a different environment and not around the stuff I had seen growing up."

Catelynn has said her relationship with April became so bad at one point that she was forced to move in with Tyler and his mother, Kim. But through the most difficult of times, her father remained one of her greatest sources of love and support. Throughout the pregnancy, he offered advice and guidance to his daughter and her boyfriend (who he didn't actually meet until 2011 during an episode of *Teen Mom*.)

"It was only him, Kim and my grandparents that supported us," Catelynn said in a 2011 interview. "Even though [MTV] didn't show it, my dad was really supportive when I was pregnant. He would tell me that I was doing the right thing and all that kind of stuff."

WHAT ABOUT TYLER?

Like Catelynn, **Tyler** knew all too well how addiction could wreak havoc on a family. His father, Butch, had been in and out of jail for most of Tyler's life. His mother, **Kim**, raised Tyler and his sister, **Amber**, single-handedly, before finally leaving Butch when Tyler was just four.

Still, Butch insists he tried to spend as much time with his children as possible. "Tyler was a riot," he remembers. "He is a Batman freak [so] we bought him a Batman suit for Halloween. He was about four, I think. When he put that mask on and that suit, he really thought he was Batman. He would hit the walls, slam the screen open. I said 'Tyler, stop.' And he says, 'I am not Tyler. I'm Batman.'"

To keep the bill collectors at bay, Kim often juggled multiple jobs, leaving little time to spend with her young children. Tyler acted out; often getting into fights at school, disrespecting authority and even earning his first suspension in the second grade.

"If he was bad and got kicked out of school for a couple of days I would take him to work with me," Butch says. "I owned a fence company and I would work 12, 14, 16 hours a day. And I would make him come work for me. I would pay him, but he didn't know he was getting paid. He would be so tired. He hated it. He rebelled a lot. He reminds me of me when I was a kid. Lookin' for attention, I assume."

Butch holds himself partly responsible for Tyler's childhood aggression and antics. "I would think [it stems] from my absence," he tells us. "I am a parent. You know, when your kids act up, you blame yourself. I wasn't there to man him up. His mother did a damn good job. But she was kind of naive. My daughter got raped when she was eight or nine years-old. I was in prison. So she blamed it on me. [Kim] had a boyfriend that raped my daughter."

The family was forced to move numerous times as money troubles mounted and Tyler continued to yearn for stability. "Before school even started, I was kicked out of all my day cares, and babysitters could not control my erratic behavior," Tyler admitted in an online posting. "My constant need for attention led me to act out as a child."

At age eight, Tyler watched as his father was tackled by police and thrown to the ground while being arrested. "All I could do was watch and cry as they took him away from me...again," he recounted. "I chased the cop car down the street until finally collapsing to my knees, and hyperventilated with tears streaming down my cheeks. Amber picked me up and we cried in the middle of the street, watching the cop car disappear in the distance for what seemed like eternity. That's when my life turned around for the worst."

EXCLUSIVE

Catelynn & Tyler's Secret Drug Arrest - Revealed!

Their secret is out!

Catelynn and Tyler were arrested for "Controlled Substance Use of Marijuana" just six days after the birth of their daughter Carly. The bust – which went down on May 25, 2009 – occurred while the young couple was still filming scenes for Catelynn's episode of *16 and Pregnant*. But it was never mentioned on the air or in the media – until now!

According to court records, the young stoners were arrested by the Marine City Police Department, fingerprinted and read their rights. Two months later, both pled guilty to the charge and each paid $253.00 in fines.

"As far as I know, they don't do any other drugs," Tyler's father, **Butch** Baltierra tells us. "But he does drink. He does party and he does smoke a lot of marijuana."

Of course, none of this partying ever made it onto TV, Butch says, because the producers and editors worked hard to hide anything that could be considered negative from the viewers.

Chapter 6

THE FARRAH YOU DIDN'T SEE ON MTV

Farrah Abraham was sobbing uncontrollably in the living room of her Hollywood, Florida apartment. Tissue in hand, the 19 year-old single mom recounted for neighbor **Alethea Montante** – who she had known for just a few short months – the heartbreaking story of how her only true love died two years earlier in a horrific car wreck. Then... "Ok, we're good!" a voice boomed from the background. "Awesome," Farrah responded, flashing a smile. "Let's go shopping!"

Farrah – a self-described "actress, author, commercial model, culinary professional, entrepreneur, professional speaker, and philanthropist" – has also become a master at the art of manipulation,

Alethea believes: "As soon as the cameras turned off, she would wipe her tears and be totally fine. She would just fake cry for the cameras."

Alethea and others who know Farrah privately describe her as a bossy diva, who would often pawn off daughter **Sophia** on friends. "How you see her act on camera isn't even close to how bad she is in person," says **Daniel Alvarez**, who dated the aspiring model during the summer of 2011 and appeared on the fourth season of *Teen Mom*. "I don't watch a lot of TV, especially not reality shows. But I wish I had watched a few episodes of *Teen Mom* before I started dating her so I could have had a heads-up on how she really was! I think sometimes she might bring it out more and embellish some of her stories for the cameras, but for the most part that's her personality. They don't make her act like that."

Alethea, a stay-at-home mom at the time, befriended her new next-door neighbor shortly after Farrah relocated from Iowa to attend The Art Institute of Ft. Lauderdale in 2011. "I was outside one day and her dad, Michael, introduced himself to me," she remembers. "He was telling me that he was worried about her living in Florida alone, so I invited him inside my house and we chatted for a while. I told him that if Farrah ever needed anything she could come over and knock on my door."

But it wasn't Farrah that eventually turned up on her front step. Within days, Alethea says, she was approached by MTV producers and asked if she would be willing to appear on camera. "I didn't even really know her, but being around celebrities doesn't really faze me, so I said OK," she recalls. "That night I did some research and read some stuff about her online that was pretty negative, about how she acts on the show and stuff. But when I met her, she was totally opposite of what I had read. She was actually really sweet. "

After just three days at the Hollywood Station apartment complex, Farrah asked if Alethea could look after Sophia for a few hours while she partied with some other neighbors at the pool. "I agreed, because she was young and I knew she would want to meet people and have some

Farrah lets loose in Austin, Texas, in 2011.

fun," she says. Little did Alethea know then that she would eventually end up watching Sophia around-the-clock, sometimes for days at a time. "On *Teen Mom*, they showed three different people watching Sophia, including me, but after a little while it had gotten to the point that I was watching Sophia all the time," she says. "Sophia would be with me all day. She was like my second child. Farrah would drop her off in the morning and not pick her up until nighttime – or sometimes the next day. I felt for her, because she was alone and young so I watched Sophia for her."

Daniel, who met the teen mom on a blind date, says he was horrified to watch as Farrah treated her daughter like a mere prop in her quest for fame. "When the cameras are there she's all about Sophia, but off camera she would dump her off to this lady that lived in her building with no heads up or anything," he confirms. Making matters worse, Sophia often needed bathing "because she stunk and was dirty," Alethea says. "But Farrah was a young mom so I gave her the benefit of the doubt. I would do everything for that little girl. I would bathe her, take her to the doctor, feed her. She was always with me." And when Alethea wasn't babysitting, she was busy dodging requests from producers to appear on camera. "It became like a job for me because they were there so often," she remembers. “Bright and early they would be there to film, even if I didn’t have my makeup on yet.”

Several friends and neighbors have told us that Farrah was a terror for her production team, reducing one crewmember to tears and prompting another to walk off the job. “She would make them wait, and talk to them so horribly,” Alethea says. “Sometimes she would make them cry because she was so mean. One of the production people actually quit because she couldn’t take Farrah anymore. She actually quit her job on the show because she didn’t want to work with her anymore.”

Daniel says the crew following him was constantly changing: “She would tell me she fired them, but in reality it was them not wanting to work with her anymore.“

Things got so bad during the filming of his third date with Farrah, that Daniel claims one of the show’s executive producers had to be called down from New York to take over for a producer who had gotten into a

Farrah with Daniel Alvarez and his parents after taping an episode of *Teen Mom*.

huge fight with the demanding star. "Farrah couldn't get along with the other producer," he said. "I saw a lot of [production/camera] people come and go and that was only in a six week period!"

Alethea was also appalled at how Farrah treated the people who tailed her for up to eight hours a day. "She didn't like me talking to the crew," she said. "She called them 'workers.' She told me, 'They work for me, I don't work for them!' She would get so mad when Michael and I would talk and MTV would film us. She would say to the production crew, 'Is this Michael's show or my show?'"

"[Farrah] didn't like me talking to the crew. She called them 'workers.' She told me 'They work for me. I don't work for them.'"

- ALETHEA MONTANTE

"If she was trying to talk to me about something, they would interject and ask her to elaborate or something, and she would just chew them out," said Daniel. "I get that it's kind of a pain, but that's what you sign up for by going on the show."

Farrah's treatment of the show's crewmembers mirrored the way she treated people in public, her former friends say. "Every time I was out with her she would either be making fun of someone or being mean to people," said Alethea. "She actually told me one time, 'You need to stay fit because I don't like fat friends!'"

John Hidalgo, another resident of the Hollywood Station apartments, says Farrah frequently spoke of "screwing people over" and recalls one time she decided to "get revenge" on a neighbor named **Adam**, who she briefly dated during the fourth season of *Teen Mom*.

"After they broke up, she got a condom and filled it with mayonnaise and put it on his doorknob," he says. "She was always doing weird things like that, to prove that she was better than people."

MTV often overlooked Farrah's treatment of those around her, and, in many cases, was forced to smooth things over with members of the general public. Daniel remembers one visit to a grocery store when Farrah encountered a cashier who struggled with her English.

"Farrah started yelling at her...telling her she shouldn't be a cashier and should be mopping the floor. I was so embarrassed that I started to walk out of the store. I couldn't believe some of the things she'd say to people," he says.

Still, many of Farrah's former friends admit that she could also be fun to hang out with. "In the beginning, we would have a lot of fun and just do normal couple things, like go to the beach, go out to eat or hang out by the pool. I was trying to show her that things aren't always bad, and not everyone is out to use her like she thought," Daniel says. "She had a lot of good qualities too. She's very ambitious and driven. She's dedicated to making money, even if she has to step on someone to do it, she will. I went into the relationship not knowing anything about Farrah or her show. I met a person that I was attracted to both physically and emotionally, and was trying to give her a chance, just like I would anybody else."

Things quickly imploded for the couple during a mid-summer trip to Daniel's hometown of Austin, Texas, he says. MTV cameras were close behind as they explored the city, lunched with Daniel's family and hung out with his friends.

"We had a really good time," he remembers. "She met my dad and stepmom and a chunk of my friends at a big dinner. MTV was there and all my friends had to sign contracts and stuff. The dinner and the parent meeting were on film. After that, the camera crew left. We went downtown to some of the bars and she ended up drinking and getting a little out of control."

Farrah with former neighbor Alethea Montante.

And that, Daniel says, is when he began to see Farrah in a different light: "I saw what most people have been seeing on TV for years – an unappreciative and self-centered individual." When their story was edited together for the final season of *Teen Mom*, it appeared that Daniel broke off the relationship rather abruptly. Not so, he says. What viewers never saw was the way Daniel says Farrah began treating his friends at a Florida nightclub.

"She was telling my friend to 'go get her another drink right now' and being really rude and demanding," he says. "Afterwards, we went to my friend's house and Farrah was disrespectful to people I've known my entire life. Finally, I told her to get out of the house and had my friend Lauren take her back to the hotel. I told her to never talk to me again."

When news of the breakup trickled back to producers, they were eager to have Daniel come back and recreate the drama for the camera. "They tried to get me to go back to the hotel and meet up with her and fight it out on camera but I wasn't having it," he says. "They even tried to stall me at the hotel so Farrah and the camera crew could come. I was standing there and saw Farrah coming around the corner and a camera crew running towards me, and just bailed. I got out of there quick."

Alethea and John both say their relationship with Farrah grew so strained that they simply decided to stop associating with her. The day she moved out of the building, "Farrah saw me in the hall and called me 'trash,'" Alethea remembers. "She was yelling at me and called the police and said that she was going to have me arrested for yelling at her. When the cops got there, they actually told her she had to leave because technically she was trespassing and didn't live there anymore. All the neighbors started clapping."

In all the commotion, John says, "one of our neighbors comes up and says that Sophia was downstairs in the car, with all the windows rolled up, screaming and crying. The neighbor said he waited 15 minutes by the car to see if Farrah would come back out, but she didn't so the neighbor went upstairs and knocked on her door and asked her if she had forgotten Sophia in the car. She said, 'Yeah, she's waiting for me.' I filmed it all on my cell phone, but didn't tell the cops because I didn't want them to take Sophia away from her."

Although his time with Farrah caused him to be publically ridiculed by *Teen Mom* fans, Daniel says he doesn't regret the experience. "I don't have any hate towards her, I'm just telling the truth," he insists. "In the long run, I look at this as a learning experience. I do not regret my time with Farrah or Sophia and am happy that I was able to be a part of their lives. I wish them both the best and hope Farrah finds happiness."

We reached out to Farrah and her mother, but both declined to be interviewed for this book. Farrah also chose not to comment on specific remarks made by Daniel, Alethea and John. Contacted by telephone, she told us: "You shouldn't talk to losers. They are all horrible people. That is why they are not in my life. They make shit up. I had to call the police on them. It wasn't even the last day. It was a lot of days. I had to call the police. I had to involve my mother. I had to get help from my family. I had to move out of my apartment building early. The building was messed up. They were selling drugs. So believe me. They don't know their ass from a hole in the ground. I discredit anything that they say because they are such mental cases."

Chapter 7

DEAR SOPHIA: A LETTER TO MY GRANDDAUGHTER

Stormie Clark desperately wants to see her granddaughter, **Sophia**. But **Farrah Abraham** has been determined not to let that happen. The two headstrong women have been locking horns in a bitter, public feud since shortly after the preschooler was born in February 2009. Stormie is still grief-stricken over the loss of her only son – Sophia's father, **Derek Underwood** – who was killed in a December 2008 car crash. Not being allowed to have a relationship with Derek's only child, she says, is "absolutely not fair" and just compounds her heartache.

Stormie, a small business owner, took Farrah to court in 2010 seeking regular visitation under a "grandparent's rights" statute. She lost after being unable to prove a pre-existing relationship with the child, who was born two months after her son's death. "Farrah wouldn't let me see Sophia so the judge ruled against me," she explained at the time. "She's a heartless, spoiled brat... If Derek were alive he'd be devastated."

Farrah had a famously tumultuous relationship with Derek. In a 2012 memoir she even admitted he died without ever being told he was Sophia's father. Still, she wrote: *"He was my first love, my only true love. We hadn't spoken in more than two months, but crazily I had still hoped we had a future together — me, him, and our baby, as one happy family."*

Farrah's book also characterized Derek as thoughtless and immature, which Stormie has vehemently denied. Now, she's finally setting the record straight, revealing for the first time that Derek's sister was also 16 and pregnant in high school, and went into labor the day of his burial. What follows is an emotional and heartbreaking letter Stormie has written to her granddaughter about the father she'll never know and the family who so desperately wants to be a part of her life.

October 12, 2012

Dear Sophia,

I am your biological grandmother, Stormie Clark. Your father, Derek Underwood was my son. He tragically died in a car accident on December 28th, 2008. I am taking this opportunity to tell you everything that you need to know about your father and why you and I are purposely being kept apart.

Right now, I am unable to see you, per your mother's and grandmother's request. We live in the same town, Council Bluffs, Iowa, literally three miles apart. There is no good reason why you and I are being separated, other than sheer selfishness and jealousy. I have wanted to be a part of your life since day one. I will never stop trying to do so.

When your mom and dad dated for approximately two-and-a-half years, your mother and I did not see eye-to-eye, due to the way that she handled their relationship. There was a lot of jealousy and control.

This is my story to you....

Derek was born on May 8, 1990. He weighed 8 lbs., 8 oz. We lived on a farm outside of St. Joseph, Missouri for several years until we moved to the city. Derek loved being on the farm. He wasn't scared of anything. He would walk right up to a cow, a snake, a dog... He was fearless. He was also allergic to any kind of bee. (This is something that you should know. You may be as well.) Derek was a very happy little boy. He always had the biggest smile on his face. He was so full of life. He was also very close to his sisters: your aunts Kassy and Alissa. They were always together, even more so when they became teenagers.

When Derek was eight, he had a dog named Jody. He was a big animal lover. Jody became sick a year and a half into her life, and she passed away right around Thanksgiving. It broke my heart to see how upset he was. He cried for two weeks over that dog.

Derek broke both bones in his left arm when he was 11. He was at a friend's house and a boy purposely threw him off a trampoline. They did surgery and put Derek's arm in a cast, and he had to stay the night at the hospital. I stayed with him until he fell asleep then quickly ran home to check on his sisters, and to take a shower and bring him a change of clothes to wear home. I felt so bad leaving him. As I headed back, a song came on the radio called "You'll Be In My Heart" by Phil Collins. And I just lost it. I cried all the way to the hospital. I told Derek about it, and from that day on, it became "our song." Whenever I heard that song, I would think of Derek. We played it at his funeral. To this day, I fall apart whenever it comes on the radio.

Derek Underwood and friend Zachary Mendoza were both killed in an automobile accident in the early morning hours of December 28, 2008. Another teenager in the car, Dustin Congdon, survived.

Derek's father and I divorced when he was eight. Derek, his sisters and I made a new start, and moved to Council Bluffs. His dad and I had made visitation arrangements to meet every other weekend. Derek's dad and I eventually remarried, and were both happy. My husband, Mike, was a wonderful stepfather to Derek and his sisters. We were very blessed to have him walk into our lives. Derek loved to fish, and would go on annual fishing trips to south Missouri with his Grandpa Neil. Derek loved anything that had to do with the outdoors. We went on several vacations to Branson, Missouri. That's where Derek met his first girlfriend.

Derek was a very handsome young man, and very popular with the ladies. He was also an amazing athlete. He played baseball right up to his senior year. He was in cross-country, wrestling, basketball. But he also loved swing choir. He wanted to play football, but I felt that it was too dangerous for him. I have filmed all of his sporting events, and would love to show them to you someday. I also have home videos of all of our holidays and school functions.

In high school, lots of girls wanted to date him. He had a few relationships, but your mom was the only girl that he had ever brought home for me to meet. She seemed sweet and was very pretty. They were a cute couple and looked very happy together.

My husband Mike and I decided to buy Derek his first car when he was 16. It was a 1996 maroon Chevy Lumina. He loved having his own car. He took your mom on lots of dates in it. They attended prom and high school sporting events together. But eventually, they began to have little arguments. I wasn't too concerned at first, but soon, I noticed some changes in Derek. He seemed quiet and distracted.

Before long, Derek was basically breaking down in tears. So we talked. His relationship with your mom was slowly going downhill. There were a few break ups that I didn't know about. Derek had finally told me that Farrah had been dating other guys when they were supposed to be together, and everything just fell apart. I remember the night when Derek called Farrah's dad and told him that Farrah was at a party and that he was concerned with what was going on there. I believe her dad called her and told her to get home.

A friend of Derek's had told me that whenever Farrah would call Derek and Derek was in his car with his friends, that he would have to stop the car, turn the radio off, shut the air conditioner off, roll all of the windows up, tell his friends to stop talking, so that Farrah could hear him without any distractions. His friend told me that happened a lot.

Derek's friends were blown away with how he had changed because of Farrah. Their relationship had become on-again, off-again. I could see that it was tearing Derek apart. His grades, school attendance, job...everything he had worked hard for was going downhill. For a while, I was even concerned about him graduating. I had finally told him that this relationship was not worth him being so emotionally exhausted. He was too young to have all of this going on.

Farrah eventually ended the relationship in the summer of 2008. Farrah's mom had her phone shut off and gave her a new cell phone so that Derek could not have any contact with her. During this time, our family had no idea that Farrah was filming 16 and Pregnant.

There were questions at their school about why these cameras were following Farrah around. Rumors flooded the high school saying that

Farrah was pregnant. Derek never mentioned anything about that to me, but my daughters told me what they had heard at school.

I was told after his death that Derek had tried many times to call Farrah and ask her if the baby was his. And each time, she said no. One of their conversations was aired on 16 and Pregnant.

During this time Derek started hanging out with the wrong crowd. He would stay out late, past his curfew. His attitude changed. His whole demeanor changed. I tried talking to him numerous times, but got nowhere. I knew that I had to step in and do something, because I could see the road he was headed down and I sensed that something bad was going to happen.

I grounded him from everything -- his car, cell phone, computer. But that only backfired and made things worse. Derek became distant and disconnected. I worked long hours at my job. I would get home around 6:00 PM and always have a house full of kids. Eventually it seemed that our house had become a "teenage sorority house." I hated how Derek's behavior had formed a wedge between us. He came and went and did his own thing. I offered family counseling to Derek but he said no.

Other family members stepped in and tried talking to him as well. It seemed as if we were all hitting a roadblock. This was all very sad for me because we have always been a tight knit family.

Christmas 2008 was like any other. We had Christmas music playing, opening our presents, watching movies and, of course, Christmas dinner. Derek and his sisters loved Christmas. They would always have lots of presents to open, even when they were teenagers. I still have not ended that tradition. I still spoil them. I could tell that Derek was putting on a smile that day, and that he was trying to hide his sadness. I could tell that he was thinking about Farrah. I felt bad for him.

After dinner, as always, Derek and his sisters went out to spend their gift cards and had a wonderful time.

Three days later....

"A day that I will never forget"

The night of December 27th, Derek came home around 7:00 PM and asked me what was for dinner. I was making chili. I asked him if he wanted any. He said no, and that he was going to go out for a bit. I said "OK. Be careful, and don't stay out too late." He said "OK," and that was the last time that I saw him.

At 3:30 AM there was a knock at our door. Everyone was sleeping. My husband, Mike, answered the door and there were two police officers standing there. The officer asked Mike if this was the residence of Derek Underwood. He answered, "Yes." The officer then asked Mike if he was Derek's father. Mike said 'No, but I am his step father, how can I help you?'

The officer then asked if Derek's mother was home. Mike said "Yes, but she's sleeping." The officer then asked Mike to go and wake me up and to tell me that he needs to speak to me. At that moment Mike knew that it was serious. Mike used to be a funeral director at his family-owned business. He invited the officers in. At first, he thought that Derek had gotten into some kind of trouble, but now realized that it was beyond that. He woke me up and I instantly thought the same thing -- that Derek had gotten into some trouble.

I walked into the living room and one of the officers asked me if I was Derek Underwood's mother. I answered "Yes." He then asked me to sit down. My heart was pounding with fear. He said that there was an accident. Your son was involved in a motor vehicle accident with two of his friends. As I stood up to get my coat to go to the hospital, he said, "Your son didn't make it."

As he spoke, it was like my brain had frozen. I just stood there in total disbelief and kept asking him over and over again what happened.

I couldn't comprehend anything that he was saying to me. I was still thinking that he was just in a car accident. He then tried explaining what had happened, but all I could see was his lips moving. My hearing had totally shut down. It was like the world had stopped and all I could hear were people talking, and saw that everyone was looking at me. I suppose I was trying to make myself believe that what he was trying to tell me wasn't real, and that this was not happening, and that nothing like this could ever happen to our family.

At this time, I saw the female officer looking at me in total despair, looking so remorseful. I heard Mike and the other officer talking about the accident. I still would not accept the fact that Derek was dead. When the officers left, Mike closed the door and tried talking to me, but I continued to be in a frozen state with a blank stare. There was no way that I was believing that my son was dead.

My first thought was to run down the street screaming "NO!!" and never turn back. I wanted to run to Derek. I had to see it for my own eyes. I also knew I had to wake the girls. Kassy was nine months pregnant and due any day. That didn't matter to me. I felt that they needed to know that there brother was gone. We gathered and fell apart together. The next thing I knew that I had to do was call Derek's dad.

I called several times but there was no answer. I started to leave a message asking him to call me and that there was an accident with one of our kids, and that is when he picked up. He asked what was going on and I told him, sobbing the whole time. I then called my mom. I asked her to call the rest of the family. I was in bed for two days. I didn't want to talk to anyone. The news reporters were at our door around the clock. I was in no shape to be giving any interviews. Alissa and Kassy said that they wanted to speak on Derek's behalf. I told them that it was up to them. Mike then asked me to help him plan Derek's visitation and funeral. Of course I didn't want to, but I knew that I had to.

Derek Underwood, age 4, with Santa Claus

He had already made all of the necessary calls, and all I needed to do was pick out a casket. I wanted the best that money could buy. I gathered music and pictures for his slideshow. Family and friends stopped by to offer their condolences. I wanted to keep the visits short because all I wanted was to be alone. Now, the holidays will never be the same.

We no longer have Derek, nor do we have you, Sophia.

I went to Kassy's doctor appointment with her to check on the baby. I had gone to every doctor's appointment with her since day one. The doctor told us that we needed to set up an appointment to schedule an induction right away for health reasons. I asked the doctor if we could wait until after Derek's visitation, which was the next day. The doctor said no, so we scheduled the induction on the morning of Derek's visitation, December 30th, 2008. I was hoping that Kassy would deliver the baby before 4:00 PM, which was when the visitation started. Kassy was still in labor during the visitation, ready to give birth at any time. I was hesitant about leaving her. I didn't want to miss the birth of my first grandchild.

Back and forth I was. I finally asked Mike to take over the visitation so I could be with Kassy. She was upset that she couldn't be at her brother's visitation. Fortunately, Ali was born after the visitation and Mike and Alissa were able to be there for her birth. When Ali was born, all I could think of was Derek and how he missed her birth by only two days. It was a bittersweet moment. He never got to meet his new baby niece. And he also never got to meet you, Sophia. I could never begin to describe how sad I am about that.

I was so mad at God for taking my son from me. But when Ali was born, I understood why everything happened the way that it did. A death, and then a birth two days later? I firmly believe that everything happens for a reason, and I believe that Ali's birth came at a time when I needed this "distraction," so to speak. That this miracle was God's way of telling me that he knew that our family was going to be going through this tragedy, and that this was the reason for Ali's early birth. Maybe I wouldn't have handled Derek's death as well if Ali hadn't been born two days after he died. For the whole next year, I secretly kept waiting for him to walk through our front door. It felt to me like he was just away in the service, and that he'd be coming home soon.

That whole week, I felt as if I had stepped outside of my body and I was a walking ghost. I was sleep deprived, overwhelmed and emotionally exhausted. On top of Derek losing his life, we now have a baby coming! I thought I would never make it. But I did. I had to. I had to find the strength to move on, and be there for Kassy and Ali.

As my world was ending, there was a new beginning for all of us. I stayed the night at the hospital with Kassy. Ali was born on a Tuesday. Derek's funeral was in Missouri, three days later. I had to make a big decision very fast, so I chose to have Derek laid to rest in St. Joseph, Missouri at the same cemetery where my father is buried.

We asked Kassy's doctor if she and the baby could travel, and he agreed only because of the circumstances. As our lives moved on with a new baby in our house, Kassy continued going to high school and graduated. We were very proud of her. When she returned to school, Kassy's friends told her that they had heard that Farrah had delivered her baby. We had no idea that Farrah was pregnant with Derek's child. Before his death, Farrah had told Derek that he was not your father.

16 and Pregnant *aired in June 2009. We were told that Farrah was on the show, and we saw the previews, so we watched it. We were shocked that they had taped Derek's voice having a phone conversation with Farrah. Although it was nice to hear his voice, it was still traumatic hearing it. We saw the episode of your mom giving birth to you. That is the first time I saw you. I said, "She looks like Derek did when he was a baby." Then I thought to myself, "Could it be?"*

From that day on, I tried reaching out to Farrah. I sent certified letters asking her to take a DNA test so that I would know for sure if you were my granddaughter. I even offered to pay for the testing. But there was no response. I have a copy of every letter that I sent.

Several months later, I received a letter from the social security office asking all of these questions about Derek and Farrah. I was floored. I had no idea why they were sending me this letter asking questions. I sat down and read it thoroughly. It basically asked me if Derek ever talked about Farrah's pregnancy with me. Or if Derek had attended any prenatal appointments with Farrah when he was alive. I answered each question honestly and sent it in. Derek never mentioned anything to me about Farrah being pregnant. It must have been because she told him that he was not the father.

When spring arrived, your Aunt Kassy, Alissa, baby Ali and I had all went to a park one day here in Council Bluffs. As we were getting out of our car, I saw you for the first time in real life. We were all so very excited to see you. You were with your babysitter. We explained our story to her, and then asked her if we could play with you and hold you. She hesitantly agreed. It was the most amazing experience holding you for the first time ever.

I could see myself in you. I could see the rest of our family. I never wanted to let you go. You seemed like a sad baby, which made me sad. Your cousin Ali was walking and talking, and you weren't able to do that yet. We even tried to help you walk down the sidewalk. But you were listless, and I became very concerned.

I took a short little walk with you. Just you and me. I carried you the whole time. I told you that I was your grandmother. I told you all about your daddy, and mostly I told you how much I loved you and wished that we could be together. After lots of hugs and kisses, we were able to get a couple of pictures, and then it was time for us to leave.

Sophia, walking away from you that day was the hardest thing that I have ever had to do. But I was very thankful that I got to at least have that moment with you that I can cherish for the rest of my life.

Oddly enough, a couple of weeks later, a man had called me, saying that he was your attorney. He asked me if I was still interested in taking a DNA test with you and your mother. I immediately said yes! He asked if I was still willing to pay for the tests. I said yes. By this time, I knew that I would have to take a DNA test in order to fight for visitation rights.

I told him that if the tests prove that you were my granddaughter, and if he really was your attorney, that I would like to see you – on a

1-26-10

Farrah,

I am writing to talk to you about Sophia. First of all, I'd like to say that she is a beautiful baby.

I have been watching the MTV show 16 + pregnant, and Teen Mom. I have also logged onto their websites, and noticed that there are pictures of you + my son Derek Underwood posted saying that he is the father of Sophia?

I would like for you + Sophia to take part in a paternity test. I need to know, for my piece of mind if Sophia is my granddaughter.

I am willing to pay for all of the testing.

I need you to call, or write me to set up the appointment. I will give you 10 days to respond.

I would like to do this the easy way, so please contact me soon.

My cell# is; [redacted]

Thank You,

Storme J. Clark

schedule that works out best for Farrah. He immediately said that he would have to ask your mother, and promised to get back with me. But he never did, which was very, very sad.

The next thing we know, Farrah sends a message to Kassy, via Facebook. Farrah hadn't talked to any of us since Derek's death. She asked Kassy to take a DNA test with her and Sophia, and said that it would be aired on the show Teen Mom.

Kassy didn't really want to be on national television, telling our story to the world. She only did it to see you. That was the only way Farrah would let anyone see you. After Kassy went on the show the couple of times that Farrah needed her to, we never heard from her again. Kassy felt betrayed and realized she was being used for ratings. Derek's dad called Farrah and asked to see Sophia. I was told by a reliable source that she only agreed to let him see Sophia if it was being filmed. He wasn't happy about that either but again, he did it only to see you.

They had filmed several times and Farrah's mother always had to be there for filming and pictures. Kassy told me that when she told Farrah that I wanted to see you, she said it was mainly her mom not wanting me to see you. There was an episode that Farrah had told her mom that Kassy wanted to start seeing Sophia, and Farrah's mom said that "we just don't have time for that".

Farrah called me out of the blue and asked me if we could have a talk at a park in Omaha. My first question was if you were going to be there. She said, "No." I asked her if there were going to be any cameras there. She had a stern voice, which I knew was not sincere. I told her that I would think about it. Moments later, I am getting phone calls from the MTV producers asking me to please talk to Farrah on camera. I haven't heard from Farrah in years and all of a sudden she wants to talk? Something was definitely brewing. A few days went by and I texted Farrah and told her that I would not be talking to her in front of cameras. I asked her to come to my house to talk. She said no.

After Farrah realized that I wasn't going along with whatever she was up to, she then sent me a very long and mean text. She basically told me that I was no longer in her life and that I would never be in your life. And that if anyone in our family tried contacting her, she would call the police and say that we were harassing her. Alissa tried calling her after reading the heartless text that she had sent me, and Farrah called the police.

I then took your mom to court to try and get grandparents' visitation rights. But the judge stated that I had to have had a substantial relationship with you in order to get visitation rights, which was very hard to do because Farrah wouldn't let me see you. Rest assured that I will never stop trying to see you, my sweet, sweet Sophia.

You are all that we have left of Derek. I sent your grandma Debra a certified letter asking her to please let me see you, when your mom went off to school in Florida. If the tables were turned, I could never keep you from them. I asked her grandmother to grandmother, to please understand what it's like not being able to see my only son's daughter. I assured her that it could be strictly by her rules, etc. She did receive that letter. I have her signature on a receipt from the post office saying that she received it. But there was still no response. Your Aunt Alissa saw you at Perkins restaurant several times with your great grandparents and talked to you briefly.

I saw you tonight outside your Grandma Debra's house. You were playing on the sidewalk and she was scooping leaves in the street. I was on my way home from work and something told me to drive by. I believe that it was your daddy telling me to. I pulled up and said: "Hi, Debra, I'm Derek's mom." The look on Grandma Debra's face instantly turned. I asked if Farrah was home. She said, "No." [Even though her car was in the driveway] She said, "You don't talk to me. Stay off of my property and get out of my face." I was in the street and not on her property. I just drove away looking at you.

You were only five feet away from me, and didn't have a clue who I was. Your Aunt Kassy and your two cousins Ali, Peyton and I came to one of Farrah's book signings in Omaha, hoping to see you, and also hoping that I could talk with Farrah.

I asked your Grandma Debra if I could take a picture of you and Ali together and she said ok. I don't really think she knew who I was, but I was so glad that I was able to get a picture.

Farrah looked busy signing her books, so I decided that we should leave and to be thankful that we got to see you, even though it was very brief. Farrah wrote a book called "My Teenage Dream Ended." There are a lot of things that I don't agree with in that book. For one, she had said that I had never even mailed you a birthday card, or birthday gifts. My thought is why would I if they would all be destroyed, and you would never see them anyway.

I have everything here at my home for when you are able to come and see me on your own, and I know that you will. I pray every day that you and your mother will stop by someday. I have been willing to work through our differences with her, but Farrah never responds.

My sweet Sophia, you have a whole other family that is dying to be a part of your life. It is so heartless of your mom and her family to keep you from us. We all love you so very much, and we will all continue to watch you on television, on whatever show you end up on, because that is the only time that we can see you. We all pray for your well being each and every day. We will be together someday, Sophia. I promise you that. I want you to know that I will never stop trying to see you.

You are and always will be my little angel from God. I love you more than you'll ever know.

- Your Grandma, Stormie

The Ashley Says...

Give Stormie A Break!

I confess: until recently, I believed that Stormie Clark was just as MTV portrayed her – a semi-crazy woman who was just trying to make Farrah's life miserable. But now I've realized she isn't crazy at all. All Stormie wants is to see her granddaughter, the last physical connection to the son she still loves so much.

It must be agonizing to know that the only way to see your grandchild is to watch her be exploited on television. As Sophia has gotten older, she has become the spitting image of her father – which has to only make things harder.

In her book, Farrah points out that Stormie was not awarded visitation because she had never really interacted with Sophia. This is true. But let's be fair: Stormie tried over and over to establish a relationship with her granddaughter, but was blocked every time by Farrah and her mom – something the show conveniently neglected to point out.

It was only when producers realized that a Farrah-Stormie feud made for good TV that they reached out to her. And when she didn't agree to appear on *Teen Mom*, Stormie was once again shunned.

Obviously, there are two sides to every story. Farrah gave her account of what happened on the show and in her book, so I'm glad that we were able to give Stormie a forum to do the same.

The real victim here is not Farrah – or Stormie – it is Sophia. She already lost her father and is now being cut off from the whole other side of her family.

If nothing else comes from this book, hopefully Farrah and her family will realize that Stormie has good intentions and allow her to finally be a part of Sophia's life.

Chapter 8

KAIL'S INCREDIBLE STORY OF SURVIVAL

Kailyn Lowry is finally getting her Happily Ever After. On September 1, 2012, the determined young mom – who has overcome bullying, an eating disorder, and abandonment by her own family – arrived at Lake Wallenpaupack, Pennsylvania expecting a low-key celebration of her one-year anniversary with boyfriend **Jose "Javi" Marroquin**. What she found instead was her son **Isaac**, 3, holding an armful of flowers and Javi, a retail clothing salesman, waiting on bended knee. As the midday sun reflected off the water, 20 year-old Kail gleefully accepted his proposal. Three days later, she married the love of her life at a small, secret ceremony in nearby Allentown.

Kail's newfound bliss comes after a lifetime of struggle and heartache. "A year after I was born, my dad just disappeared," the newlywed remembers. "One night he just never came home. I'd ask my mom about him and she would tell me that she didn't know where he was." Kail, an only child, was born just one year after her mother, **Suzi Irwin**, married rancher **Ray Lowry** in Tarrant County, Texas. "My mom said [her pregnancy] was planned," she says. "My dad said it wasn't."

No Support From Mom

By the time Kail was out of diapers, her parents' young marriage had fallen apart, and Suzi, a part-time bartender, found herself dependent on booze to get through each day. "Growing up, I never had a real relationship with my mom," Kail acknowledges. "I'd have to parent her when she was on her binges. She was a binge drinker and you never knew what she was going to do. My mom's best friend was a drinker and a drug user also. She had six daughters, so I'd always be over there with them while our moms went out and did their thing."

A former high school lacrosse star – who grew up with dreams of becoming a dentist – Kail spent much of her childhood in the vicinity of Honesdale, Pennsylvania, bouncing around from home to home as her mom transitioned from one boyfriend to the next. "I moved four different times [and went to] four different schools," she recalls. "In elementary school, I had a lot of friends and everyone knew each other. The town that I'm from is really small, like 1,500 people, so

Kail Lowry, age 5

everyone knows each other. Then, in fifth grade, I moved again and I had to go to a new school. They weren't really fond of new people. I was bullied a lot. I got picked on a lot."

Through it all, Kail never let her grades suffer. She participated in numerous after school activities, but even then, received little attention from her mother. "I did cheering for a few years." she says. "That was probably the most active she ever was with me. She would come to competitions."

As Kail struggled to gain acceptance in middle school, Suzi checked into an inpatient alcohol treatment center, signing custody of her daughter over to a neighbor. "At the time, I was close to [the family], so that was good," Kail remembers. "But I don't really think they wanted me there. I think they just felt bad. It wasn't always comfortable; I shared a room with one of their kids. I really just felt like I was wearing out my welcome — and it wasn't my choice."

Rocky Road With Jo

By the time Suzi returned from the first of her many stints in rehab, Kail had begun to battle demons of her own. "When I was in middle school, I had a really hard time being called the 'chunky girl,'" she revealed to *Wetpaint.com*. "I would go on bouts where I wouldn't eat or try to make myself throw up." Sadly, her mother never noticed. But after transferring to Nazareth Area High School in the tenth grade, Kail did catch the attention of aspiring Latino rapper **Jonathan "Jo" Rivera**, while dining at a local McDonalds. Rivera attended rival Easton High School, but football rivalries weren't going to get in the way of raging teenage hormones.

"I guess I was attracted to him because he was from a different culture than I was," Kail admits. "Where I grew up everyone was white, so that was different. He also had a really solid family, so those are the two things I really remember being attracted to him for." The couple began to date and soon became serious. "His grades started to slip...and his parents didn't like that and didn't really want him seeing me anymore," Kail remembers.

Despite the disapproval, the young lovers continued their forbidden romance. They went on dates to the movies and the local roller skating rink. In time, Kail grew close to Jo's parents, **Janet** and **Eddie**, and his brother, Eddie Junior. Her relationship with Jo, however, soon began to unravel. "Really early into it we were fighting and we would break up off and on," she says. Then, nine months into their turbulent courtship, Kail made a mistake with her birth control that would change both of their lives. "I was on the pill but I wasn't taking it correctly," she admits. "Like, I'd miss three days and then take three pills and think that it would make up for it, stuff like that. I didn't have a way to get the pill without my mom knowing, and I didn't really know how to use it correctly."

On the night of Jo's senior prom, in May 2009, Kail arrived at the Rivera house dressed in a sparkly, bright blue gown she had purchased using money from her after-school job at a Hallmark card store. She posed for photos with Jo before heading out to the dance. Hours later Kail and Jo had unprotected sex and suddenly Kail was 16 and pregnant.

"I never actually missed my period," she says. "I remember about a week before [it was due], I woke up and I just kind of thought, 'I'm pregnant and I know it.' So I went and got a test and it came out positive. I couldn't really believe it. I called Jo and told him, 'You need to come over here and see this. I need to show you something.' So he came over and took one look at the positive test and just left. He didn't know what to say. He just got in his car and left. I think he needed time to process it all."

And Baby Makes Three

"Growing up, I had seen girls with baby bellies and babies and I'd always think, 'How is that girl going to go to school with a baby?'" Kail remembers. "So that's how I felt when I got pregnant... Like, 'how am I going to continue my education?'" For months, the nervous teen tried to hide her pregnancy from friends and family. When Jo eventually told his parents, "Janet sat me down on the bed and told me, 'It's OK if you want to get an abortion, because you guys are so young,'" she recalls. "She was basically telling me to get an abortion. I still have resentment for that." The exchange wasn't mentioned in Kail's *16 and Pregnant* episode, though Janet appears in one scene expressing her feeling that they were too young to handle a baby.

"Janet sat me down on the bed and told me, 'It's OK if you want to get an abortion, because you guys are so young,' She was basically telling me to get an abortion. I still have resentment for that."

- KAIL LOWRY

The news didn't go over any better at Kail's house. Fearing the worst, she never even told her mother about the pregnancy. "I always grew up saying that my mom would never know her grandchildren," she explains. "I just kind of felt that she didn't deserve to know... But she had a feeling because she would drive me to school and I'd always make her pull over so I could throw up. She found out by hearing it around town I guess. When she finally did confront me about being pregnant, she was piss drunk and I just didn't respond at all."

But Suzi's boyfriend did. He promptly kicked Kail out of the house, as her mother, whose name was on the lease, looked on, offering no support. "She just said 'You're going to be on your own,'" Kail remembers. "She never offered to help me or anything." For the second time in her life, Kail found herself essentially homeless. When Jo's family agreed to take her in, Suzi was quick to sign over custody for the second time in three years. “His parents weren’t thrilled but they knew the situation with my mom and figured this was for the best,” Kail says.

After settling into Jo’s room at the Rivera family’s nearly 4,000 square foot house, Kail began to take stock of her options. Abortion was never a consideration, she says. But adoption was. Ultimately Kail decided to keep her baby – mainly because she believed that Jo and his family “would always be there financially to support the baby.”

Kail Gets Her Close Up

During her first trimester, Kail – like so many other young girls – went online and found a casting notice for *16 and Pregnant*. “I wanted to do [the show] because there were six girls on the first season, and five of them had their parents behind them and supporting them – all of them except Catelynn,” she says. “I didn’t have that. I didn’t have a dad. My mom was a crazy addict, so I thought people could benefit from my story since it wasn’t like the rest of the girls’.”

Within weeks, casting directors from MTV and 11th Street Productions came calling. Surprisingly, Suzi agreed to show up for the first round of interviews and offered her blessing. She wasn’t, however, required to sign any of the official paperwork, because the Riveras were now Kail’s legal guardians. Three months later, a six-man production crew was on their doorstep. “I don’t think people actually knew I was pregnant,” Kail says. They might have just thought I was fat.”

Cameras trailed the usually shy mother-to-be all around town as she shopped for baggy clothes to hide her quickly growing baby bump. But the local Board of Education wouldn’t allow MTV crews past the front door of her high school. As word of the production spread, people who had never spoken to Kail before were suddenly trying to become her new best friend. “People definitely treated me different because I was on the show,” she says. “To this day I still feel like they do.”

Reconnecting with Dad

As Kail coped with her newfound fame at school, she decided to make one last attempt to smooth things over with her father, who had since resurfaced back in Texas. Prior to being officially selected for the show, she was contacted through *Facebook* by an aunt she hadn't seen in more than a dozen years. After several conversations, Kail agreed to fly south in November 2009 to meet a handful of extended family members, and reconnect with the man who turned his back on her years earlier. MTV sent its camera crew along to document the emotional and awkward reunion. Kail hoped the trip would make her father want to be the parent she never had. Unfortunately, that's not how it played out.

"Even though he was my dad, he was still a complete stranger to me," she says. "I had no idea who this person was, so I guess I wanted to meet him because I was curious and I needed closure. When I got there, things were just weird." Ray, who was full of stories about road kill and kept a lock on his refrigerator to protect his supply of meat, was not exactly the stable father Kail had hoped for. "They didn't show it on camera, but right after I got there, my dad asked me to borrow $20," she remembers. "That really pissed me off because, come on, I'm a pregnant 16-year-old girl! Why are you asking to borrow money? Supposedly he has like two Associates degrees, but he doesn't have a job and he's a moocher, so I didn't need him in my life. I've been fine without him, but I wanted to meet him to get closure." Kail has not seen her father since.

Welcoming Isaac

Two months after the trip, Kail went into labor. "Jo and Janet worked in New Jersey, so that morning they had already left by the time my water broke at about 5 AM," she remembers. "I thought I had peed my bed!" Alone at Jo's house without anyone nearby that she could call, Kail was forced to reach out to her mother for help. Five hours later, Suzi finally arrived. "She came over about 10 am and sat with me and then she realized that I was in labor and took me to the doctor," Kail says. "If I could go back and do it again I wouldn't have allowed her to have any part in it at all. I got lucky and she was sober when it happened, because she's really crazy and could have been really drunk."

At the hospital, things get chaotic extremely fast. Her tiny hospital room was packed with family, friends and intrusive cameras. "I remember telling one of the [producers] – who I had just met for the first time – to 'get the fuck out of my face' during one of my contractions," she says. "I remember everyone talking and wanted to be like six inches from my face. I would have a contraction and I just wanted it to be quiet but it wasn't. When I gave birth there were two camera people, the executive [producer], a production assistant, the doctor, Jo, Janet, my mom, and like four of my friends in the room with me. My friends came in because they figured that there were already so many people there that it didn't matter. So that's like 15 people. It wasn't really a private moment, and it wasn't special, with so many people there it couldn't be."

Isaac Elliott – whose name was misspelled on Kail's episode – was born on January 18, 2010. After his birth, Jo tried to make up for the way he treated his girlfriend during the pregnancy. "He could be really sweet and caring," she says. The couple briefly became engaged, but soon encountered a new set of problems -- including a lack of privacy while living with the Riveras. "I felt like sometimes his parents would try to overpower us and raise Isaac the way they wanted him to be raised," Kail says. "I think [Jo] being so close to his parents and me being used to being so independent caused a lot of problems in our relationship. I wasn't used to having anyone monitoring what I was doing."

She also wasn't accustomed to having an audience of millions analyzing her relationship and parenting choices on television. The overall experience with her episode of *16 and Pregnant* "pissed me off," she says. "I put my whole life out there, and they can't even bother to spell my son's name right?" Nevertheless, she eventually accepted an offer to continue her story on the spinoff *Teen Mom 2*. And after a little prodding, a reluctant Jo signed on, too.

The camera crews returned in June 2010, just as Kail and Jo's relationship began to flat line. This time the couple split for good and before long, Kail struck up a romance with coworker **Jordan Wenner**. That didn't sit well with Jo or Janet, who she once referred to as "a second mother." By December 2010, Kail had moved out of the Rivera family basement, where she had been living after she and Jo had broken up, and into an apartment of her own.

"I think Janet was very hurt and upset with how I left," Kail says. "I think she is still upset about it." Kail says she felt bad, too, despite the fact that season one episodes of *Teen Mom 2* were edited to make it seem like she didn't. That Christmas, Kail wrote Janet a heartfelt letter, thanking her for all she had done. They tried to further smooth things over during the season one reunion special, which was taped in February 2011. But by then, things had gotten so bad with Jo that Kail refused to tell him where she and his son were living. Though viewers didn't get to see most of it, the couple had a huge blowup on stage while taping a segment with Janet and **Dr. Drew Pinsky**. Eyewitnesses say things got particularly heated when Jo criticized Kail for not telling him that she was dating Jordan, and continuing to hook up with him. Kail, in turn, revealed that Jo had cheated on her while she was pregnant -- with a 25 year old! Janet stepped in, aided by a team of MTV staffers, to try and stop the angry couple from airing any more dirty laundry.

But for Kail, the real damage was done long ago. By participating on *Teen Mom 2*, she has already exposed her most intimate moments to millions of judgmental viewers. She's also watched her private life – including reports Jo gave her a sexually transmitted disease, accusations she smoked marijuana during pregnancy, and rumors about multiple lesbian affairs in high school -- play out in tabloid headlines. So it's no wonder Kail was concerned that Javi might be nervous about putting his life on public display, too.

"At first I think he was a little apprehensive about dating me and being on the show," she admits. Kail also reveals that MTV tried to make it look as if they were set up by mutual friends at a bowling alley, but their introduction really came while she was working at a retail clothing store called Buckle in the Lehigh Valley Mall. "Javi and his brother come in. I assume his older brother is his dad and that gets us laughing," she recounts on her personal website. "Javi lies to me about what he was shopping for... I eventually learn that he hates graphic tees. At check out he asks to take me for ice cream and I tell him 'No.' LOL. Hard to see that looking back I turned him down! Anyway, from there he came into Buckle again and we started forming a friendship via *Twitter* and Buckle visits. Eventually, I gave him my number." Kail reveals she tried to keep the relationship from MTV producers for months, "but then he started to become such a big part of my life that we couldn't hide it any longer. After a while, I had to tell them about him."

Kail's relationship with Javi soon became serious, and the couple moved in together in 2012. However, the relationship hit a speed bump in the spring of 2012, when a fight between Kail and Javi escalated. The fight, which started due to a disagreement Kail and Javi were having in regards to filming, resulted in a frustrated Kail screaming and pushing Javi. MTV cameras captured the incident for an episode for the fourth season of *Teen Mom 2*.

"I felt like so many things were out of control and I didn't know how to handle that," Kail told *Wetpaint.com*. "There was a moment where I take Javi's head and I shook it. I had a temper so bad, that I knew I was getting out of control."

Although Javi quickly forgave her for the incident, Kail says she knew she had to seek help for the mental health issues she had been avoiding facing. Kail had known for a while before the incident that she, like her mother, suffered from bipolar disorder. However Kail had avoided getting treatment for the disorder because she didn't want to believe. After the fight with Javi, Kail knew she had to get help and is now seeing a therapist and taking medication.

When a clip of the incident was shown during the *Teen Mom 2* season four trailer, Kail decided to address what had happened.

"Even though Javi and I have moved on from it, I want to say I'm sorry again to him and his family for letting my emotions get the best of me," she told *Starcasm.net* in February 2013. "I know how humiliating that is for them and I'm humiliated myself."

In late 2012, after Kail and Javi had become husband and wife, Javi joined the U.S. Air Force and left for basic training. Kail says she's confident that she's finally found the right partner in Javi. The couple, who briefly reunited in February 2013 when Javi graduated from basic training, will spend more time apart before eventually settling on a military base.

In March 2013, Kail celebrated her 21st birthday by taking a trip to West Virginia to visit **Leah**. (**Chelsea** also made the trip.) However, there would be no night of crazy partying and birthday shots to ring in her big day. Just weeks before her birthday, Kail had received the big news that she was pregnant! She had conceived during the weekend of Valentine's Day, when she had flown to Texas to join Javi at his boot camp graduation.

While the pregnancy certainly threw a curveball in the newlywed's future plans, Kail and Javi are ecstatic about their unexpected addition. However, the producers of *Teen Mom 2* didn't exactly share the couple's happiness. Having yet another one of its stars become pregnant again didn't, in the producers' eyes, relay the right message of preventing pregnancy in teens and young adults, and they were upset.

Still, Kail, who is due in November 2013, says she refuses to let anyone take away her and her husband's happiness. Instead, she is focusing on enjoying the moment.

The Ashley Says...

Kail's Not 16 Anymore!

The show is still called *Teen Mom 2*, but Kail is all grown up. She's married and has a stable living situation. Although many of the show's fans (and apparently its producers) have negative things to say about Kail becoming pregnant again, it's fairly common for couples in the military to have their children at a young age. Plus, Kail's son is getting older and it's likely that she wants to keep all of her children close in age so that they can grow up together.

Kail has always been the most level-headed of the *Teen Mom 2* cast, so if she thinks she can handle another baby, more power to her!

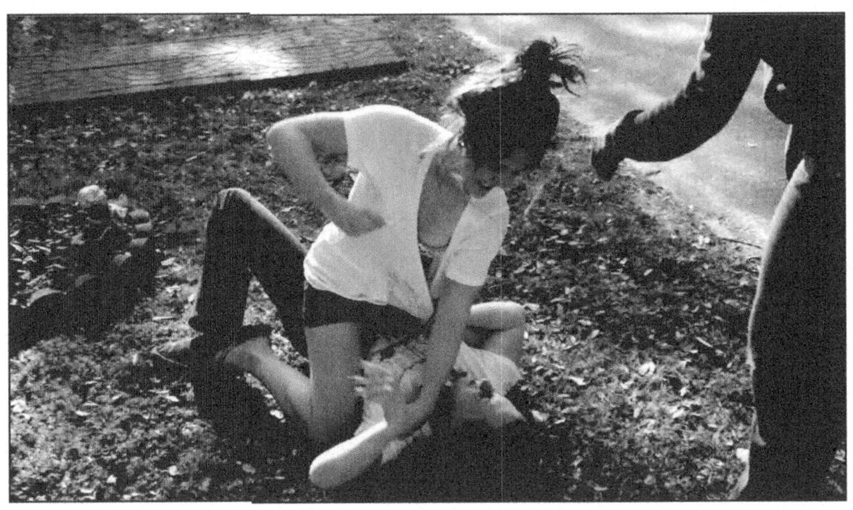

Chapter 9

JENELLE'S WILD & CRAZY LIFE: A TIMELINE

Y.O.L.O., **Jenelle**! Two engagements, eight arrests, a marriage, separation, boob job and who knows how many tattoos.... Baby **Jace**'s pot-smoking, trash-talking mom has already crossed a lifetime's worth of dubious accomplishments off her bucket list – and she just turned 21 in December 2012.

Miss any of the headline-grabbing goodness? Here's a quick recap of Jenelle's most memorable moments:

December 19, 1991: Jenelle is born in Scranton, Pennsylvania to **Robert** and **Barbara Evans**. Her dad abandons the family when Jenelle is just three years old. Barbara works two or three jobs at a time to support their three children.

2004: Barbara moves the family from Pennsylvania to North Carolina.

September 26, 2006: Sister **Ashleigh** is arrested for physically assaulting Barbara and Jenelle. Per the official arrest report: "Ms. Evans reported that her daughter Ashleigh had assaulted her. Ms. Evans said Ashleigh has mental problems and has not been taking her medication. Ashleigh got out of control and assaulted Ms. Evans and her younger sister."

March 3, 2007: Brother **Colin** is picked up on two charges: Injury to Personal Property and Injury to Real Property after a fight with Barbara. "Upon receiving a report of a domestic disturbance, I arrived to find Barbara Evans and her son Collin [sic] arguing in the front yard," the arresting officer wrote. "Ms. Evans stated that Mr. Evans had been in an altercation with her boyfriend [Mike] and punched and kicked [Mike's] truck. [He also] shattered the front glass storm door." Colin, who reportedly suffers from bipolar disorder, had been living at a group home at the time of the incident.

December 28, 2007: Barbara calls the cops when Jenelle runs away from home. According to the official police report, she said her daughter "became upset after she confronted her about being impaired" and she "did not know where Jenelle was going but stated that she left on foot." After police canvass the neighborhood, Jenelle is found at the home of her boyfriend, **Andrew Lewis**.

October 14, 2008: Andrew's mom calls the cops, claiming Jenelle broke into her house. Jenelle is arrested when she refuses to leave. According to police records, Jenelle "continued to refuse to leave, even after her mother attempted to take her home." Jenelle is arrested and released with no bail. The report says: "Victim doesn't wish to prosecute, but [Jenelle] must not come to house uninvited and leave at reasonable hour."

Late 2008: Jenelle, now working at an Irish bar, sleeps with co-worker **Stephen Fullwood** – who is dating her BFF, **Tori Rhyne**. Their mutual friend **Kaylin Zorich** tells *Star* magazine that Jenelle fears Stephen might be Jace's father, but doesn't want Tori to know they hooked up. Meanwhile, Andrew – Jace's real dad – is in rehab.

August 6, 2009: Jace is born, weighing in at six pounds, four ounces. Jenelle is in labor for 12 hours.

February 16, 2010: Jenelle's episode of *16 and Pregnant* kicks off the show's second season.

June 10, 2010: Jenelle signs over primary legal and physical custody of Jace to her mother. (In December 2012, Jenelle revealed on *Twitter* that Child Protective Services gave her an ultimatum to either sign over custody to her mother, or place Jace in foster care.)

Fall 2010: Jenelle meets **Kieffer Delp** through mutual friends.

ARREST #1 - Oct. 15, 2010: Jenelle and Kieffer are arrested for breaking and entering in Oak Island, North Carolina. The house belonged to the mother of one of their friends. Jenelle is also charged with drug possession and possession of paraphernalia. She is released on a $2,000 bond and is eventually sentenced to 12 months of probation and required to submit to monthly drug tests.

November 21, 2010: Barbara commits Jenelle (involuntarily) to Brunswick Community Hospital. Reports say she "was found not to be a threat to herself or anyone else." Jenelle is released early the next morning.

December 29, 2010: Jenelle's baby daddy, Andrew Lewis, is arrested for not paying $824 in child support.

January 11, 2011: *Teen Mom 2* premieres.

ARREST #2 - March 27, 2011: Jenelle is back in police custody with misdemeanor charges of assault and affray. She was caught on tape pummeling former friend **Brittany Truett**, after a disagreement over boyfriend **Kieffer Delp**.

Early April 2011: Jenelle gets into another physical fight, this time with friend and roommate, Tori Rhyne, while filming an episode of *Teen Mom 2*. No charges are filed.

April 2011: Jenelle's one-year probation begins. During this time, she is unable to "use, possess or control any illegal drug or controlled substances unless prescribed for the defendant by a licensed physician," according to court records.

May 7, 2011: Jenelle voluntarily heads to a drug treatment rehab center in Malibu, California. Much of her 30-day stay is filmed for *Teen Mom 2*. "She's actually excited about going to rehab," Jenelle's' friend, **Patrick Williams**, tells *OK!* magazine. "She wants this. She wants to grow up."

July 13, 2011: Jenelle violates the terms of her probation by testing positive for THC (found in marijuana). She's also behind on payments to the court and hasn't attended required aftercare since being released from rehab. According to her official violation report: "The defendant tested positive for THC on 7/13/2011 and admitting to using same. The defendant was discharged from inpatient drug treatment on 6/7/2011 and recommended aftercare/discharge plan was not followed. Since the defendant's discharge from inpatient treatment she has failed to follow up with any aftercare."

July 17, 2011: *TMZ* posts photos of Jenelle smoking and posing with marijuana, two days after failing her drug test.

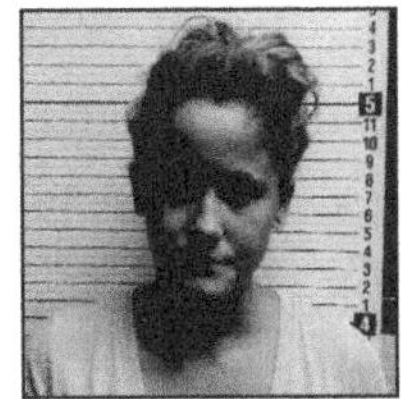

ARREST #3 - August 8, 2011: Jenelle is again behind bars in North Carolina after testing positive for marijuana and opiates (another violation of her probation). She is eventually released on $10,000 bond.

September 6, 2011: Jenelle's mom calls the police on her daughter after they get into a fight. "On September 6, 2011 I received a call from dispatch in reference to a domestic," the responding officer wrote in the police report. "I spoke to the caller, Barbara Evans, who stated her daughter, Jenelle Evans, started cursing at her, calling her names, and was destroying the residence." Barbara did not press charges.

November 22, 2011: Jenelle upsets close friend and *Teen Mom 2* co-star Kail Lowry when she attempts to make a date for a weekend getaway with Kail's ex-boyfriend, **Mike Lush**. "That's the last time I will ever defend someone who is consistently talked about," Kail tweets after finding out. "What hurts the most is I always said we were closest...no good deed goes unpunished."

January 3, 2012: Jenelle begins dating Marine **Gary Head**.

January 5, 2012: Photos showing Jenelle drinking and partying with Tori Rhyne are posted on *Twitter*. They were reportedly taken by her former boss, **James Duffy**, in November 2011 – while Jenelle was on probation.

ARREST #5 - January 10, 2012: Still on probation for beating the bejesus out of Brittany Truett, Jenelle is booked into Brunswick County (North Carolina) Jail – this time for making "harassing phone calls" and "communicating threats"

to former roommate **Hannah Inman**. Her attorney, **Dustin Sullivan**, calls the charges "absurd and retaliatory in nature." She is sprung after posting a $1,000 bond, later tweeting: "I'm free as a biiirrrrddddd :D."

ARREST #6 - January 16, 2012: Jenelle is behind bars for the second time in a week after North Carolina cops pick her up for violating a domestic violence protective order, which forbid her from contacting Hannah. She is again released on $1,000 bail.

February 14, 2012: Jenelle spends the night in the hospital, reportedly for a tonsillectomy and dehydration.

March 5, 2012: Jenelle is arrested on charges of cyber-stalking her former boss, James Duffy. She turns herself in and is released from jail after spending less than a half hour behind bars.

April 4, 2012: Tori Rhyne tells *Star* magazine that Jenelle uses LSD, Ecstasy tablets, Xanax, Adderall and alcohol. "Jenelle has been clean and sober since July of last year and has successfully completed each and every random drug test that was given to her every week for nearly eight months," Jenelle's lawyer, **Dustin Sullivan**, tells *Today.com*.

April 16, 2012: Tori Rhyne tells *RadarOnline* that Jenelle is a cutter! "They're all crazy," she says of the Evans family. "It just messed with her head."

April 16, 2012: Gary reveals on *Twitter* that he proposed to Jenelle – and she accepted! But later that day, Gary says he found out that Jenelle had been talking to her ex-boyfriend, Kieffer, and had paid for him to come visit her in North Carolina. Gary breaks off the engagement.

May 2, 2012: Kieffer and an MTV camera crew tag along for Jenelle's breast augmentation surgery.

May 8, 2012: *RadarOnline* posts nude photos of Jenelle from both before and after her boob job. Kieffer later admits he leaked them.

May 16, 2012: Jenelle announces her engagement to Gary, weeks after they broke up and got back together.

June 7, 2012: Jenelle and Gary storm **James Duffy**'s house – allegedly with a gun – to retrieve a pair of Jenelle's panties that he had been posting photos of on his *Twitter* account.

ARREST #7 - June 24, 2012: Jenelle claims Gary tried to strangle her with a bed sheet. He is arrested on domestic violence charges, but Jenelle is also picked up after police find drugs and drug paraphernalia at their residence. She is charged with possession of drug paraphernalia, marijuana possession, and possession of a controlled substance. Both spend the night in jail and are released the next morning.

July 2012: Ashleigh tells *Star* magazine that Jenelle stole $500 from her. A bitter feud ensues.

July 19, 2012: Jenelle announces that she and Kieffer are living together again.

August 20, 2012: Graphic nude photos of Jenelle – which she claims were taken by James Duffy – show up on *Twitter*.

August 28, 2012: Jenelle's charges from her June 2012 arrest are dropped. Gary pleads guilty to assault.

September 2012: Barbara stages an intervention for her daughter. She and her boyfriend, Mike, reportedly go to the Delp house in New Jersey to pick up Jenelle after hearing reports that she is using heroin. Kieffer has Barbara and Mike arrested and charged with second degree trespassing.

September 20, 2012: Jenelle is hospitalized in New Jersey for what she calls a "ruptured cyst." (It is rumored that she is actually detoxing from heroin.) While there, she tweets that she and Kieffer are no longer together.

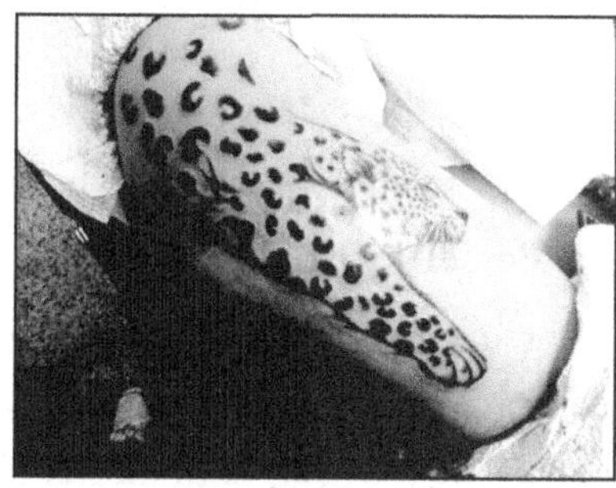

October 1, 2012: Jenelle gets a giant leopard print tattoo on her thigh. Why? "The Leopard itself represents how strong I am but no one knows and they underestimate my strength so that's why the leopard print fades away," she writes on her *Sulia* page. "I'm so strong and no one sees, I guess no know one sees my strengths because I do it discretely. It's very hard to explain my tattoo but I know what it means. I hope you guys understand, lol."

October 10, 2012: Jenelle begins dating 26 year-old **Courtland Rogers**. They are reportedly introduced by a drug dealer.

November 5, 2012: Jenelle is hospitalized again, this time in New York City. "Yayyy! Another ruptured cysssst!" she tweets. "NICE, ughhh... In soooo much pain :'(" [sic]

November 19, 2012: Jenelle and Courtland announce that they are engaged during an online chat. Fans are alarmed by Jenelle's haggard and thin appearance, spurring rumors that she is abusing drugs.

November 23, 2012: Ashleigh tells *Star* magazine that Jenelle was involuntarily committed into the Old Vineyard Behavioral Health Hospital in Winston-Salem, North Carolina. "My mom first realized Jenelle was doing heroin when she walked into her house a month ago and saw her." Jenelle tells fans she was having cyst-related surgery.

November 26, 2012: Allison Lester – a friend and roommate who accompanied Jenelle to New York weeks earlier – publicly accuses her of using heroin. "She's an addict, end of story," Allison tweets, adding that Jenelle also uses the drug Suboxone.

December 4, 2012: Jenelle and Courtland marry in the magistrate's office of the Brunswick County courthouse, moments after the groom is charged with a felony for obtaining property under false pretenses.

December 10, 2012: A video is posted on YouTube that includes a phone conversation in which Barbara openly discusses Jenelle's heroin use with Kieffer's mother.

December 17, 2012: Jenelle posts a photo on *Twitter*, showing a text she sent to her mother. It reads: "Yeah that's what happens when u commit me to the hospital...becuz u like to have things your way." [sic]

December 19, 2012: Jenelle celebrates her 21st birthday.

December 30, 2012: After Jenelle accuses her husband of 26 days of talking to **Taylor Lewis** – the mother of his infant daughter – behind her back, she tells her *Twitter* followers that she is "done" with Courtland.

December 31, 2012: Jenelle and Courtland reconcile and head to a North Carolina club to celebrate on New Year's Eve.

January 16, 2013: Courtland confirms to *Star* magazine that Jenelle is pregnant with her second child. "Me and Jenelle are so happy that she's pregnant," he says. "She told me 'I'm looking forward to a second chance.'" Later in the day, Jenelle tells MTV that she "missed a few birth control pills" and got the news during a doctor's appointment. "I was really surprised," she says. "I know a lot of people will say we're not ready, or judge me from my past. I want to prove to everyone that I can do this. This wasn't planned, but it happened so we're taking it as we go. Courtland and I are happy and excited now. We have our own place, we're married, and we're both working. We know having a child can be difficult, but we're going to do our best."

January 17, 2013: *RadarOnline* publishes Jenelle's sonogram photos, and Jenelle uploads a photo of her stomach to *Instagram* with the caption: "Baby bumpppp. My little angel!" She reveals that her due date is September 4, 2013.

January 21, 2013: Jenelle and Courtland are once again at each other's throats after Courtland leaves his pregnant wife alone to go party with his friends. She accuses him of cheating on her. Courtland denies the claim on *Twitter*: "I went out last night and got wasted and came home at 3 am and I left my pregnant wife asleep by herself but I didn't cheat!! I just left." Jenelle insists that she's divorcing him. She pays a visit to her ex-fiance Gary Head later that night.

January 22, 2013: Jenelle claims she was rushed to the hospital. Later that day, the administrator of her *Facebook* fan page updates fans on her condition: "Jenelle's conditions are not good, but cannot say more about what happened. Pray for her and the baby and also that certain people get what they deserve. She is very hurt and feels very betrayed."

January 23, 2013: Jenelle, fresh out of the hospital, blasts Courtland on *Twitter*: "I am getting a divorce, ASAP. YOU F**KING LEAVE OUT OF TOWN AND I MIGHT BE HAVING A MISCARRIGE?! F**K U, U F**KING PIECE OF SH*T." Hours later, Jenelle's attorney, **Dustin Sullivan**, confirms that she has filed four charges of assault on a female with an unborn child against her husband. It's reported that Jenelle's skull had been fractured as a result of him hitting her. Courtland, who had fled the state by the time the charges were filed, tells *RadarOnline* "I did not hit my wife. This is not true at all."

January 24, 2012: Courtland appears on *Stickam* and declares that he and Jenelle made $20,000 for selling the story of her pregnancy to *Star* magazine. He also claims the baby might not be his, and says she cheated on him with a guy named Kris. Courtland insists he never hit Jenelle and that she bruised her own cheek. He also says that, despite her pregnancy, "she's still getting high. She's doin' all types of sh*t...Right now she's doin' pain pills, Xanax and smokin' weed."

January 25, 2013: While staying at Gary Head's house, Jenelle fears she is having a miscarriage and rushes to the hospital. Later that day, a friend tells *RadarOnline* that, "Jenelle lost the baby this morning. She's sad and upset, but she'll make it through." Gary and Jenelle continue to tweet from the hospital, even posting photos of her hospital room. Gary insists that he and Jenelle are not romantically involved and that they are just friends. Courtland arrives at the hospital, but is turned away after he is told that Jenelle doesn't want him there. Later that night, Jenelle, Gary and friends hit the town, hanging out at several bars and posting photos of themselves online.

January 26, 2013: Courtland rants on *Facebook*: "supposedly beat her and she just lost our baby 2 hours ago but all of a sudden there's no marks on her and she is taking Gary shopping... I am happy to screen shot that pic of her in the mirror singing she just took after losing our baby due to Xanax use!! I cannot wait to go to court and show this judge the truth about her she needs to learn that he is not the f***ing president and that she can't just make up some sh!t to destroy someone's life!"

February 6, 2013: Courtland, still wanted on assault charges (filed by Jenelle), turns up in a South Carolina hospital. It's reported that he is there to detox off of drugs. He tells *RadarOnline*, "I've been under suicide watch and I don't even have shoelaces. All I want is my wife back. Jenelle is my best friend and I miss her." Courtland's baby-momma Taylor tells fans on *Twitter* that Courtland will remain in the hospital for a week before turning himself into police.

February 11, 2013: Jenelle's baby daddy, Andrew Lewis, appears on the *Teen Mom 2* season three reunion special and admits that he was physically abusive during their relationship.

February 12, 2013: Jenelle and her ex, Gary Head, announce that they are officially back together – despite the fact that she is legally still married to Courtland.

February 25, 2013: MTV reportedly sends Jenelle to rehab in Florida. "[Jenelle] is seeking treatment for her drug addiction issues and related stresses stemming from her tumultuous last few months," a source tells *RadarOnline*. The website claims that Jenelle went to the treatment facility willingly.

March 1, 2013: Jenelle and Gary Head split. That same day, she is released from rehab and immediately starts lashing out at Gary on *Twitter*.

March 5, 2013: Jenelle checks into another rehab facility. "Jenelle was in great spirits before she went in," a source told *RadarOnline*. "She is really hoping that she can get control of her life. She is bi-polar and she's had a really hard time balancing the medication she needs for that."

March 6, 2013: Courtland Rogers is arrested in North Carolina for his outstanding warrants, stemming from the abuse charges that Jenelle filed against him.

March 10, 2013: Jenelle returns to her social media accounts, posting that she is once again out of rehab. Her stay lasted only lasted four days.

Late March, 2013: Jenelle and Courtland get back together and try to rekindle their romance.

ARREST #8 - April 23, 2013: Jenelle is taken into custody (again) when North Carolina's finest catch her with 12 bindles of heroin. She is also charged with assaulting Courtland.

April 24, 2013: Jenelle is kicked out of Courtland's house by his mother.

The Ashley Says...

Jenelle's Real Addiction Is Fame

She's gone to rehab twice on MTV's dime – both reportedly for drug-related addiction issues – but there's only one thing, in my opinion, that Jenelle is addicted to: fame. She feeds off of the notoriety she's garnered from appearing on MTV. When something goes wrong in her life (or whatever relationship she's in at the moment), Jenelle makes a beeline for *Twitter*. She seeks validation from her 700,000-plus followers, but, sadly, more than half of them are probably only following her to watch the train wreck.

Jenelle's antics onscreen pale in comparison to her social media activity, essentially turning the show into a mockery of itself. It's quite ridiculous to watch an episode of *Teen Mom 2* that was filmed nearly a year ago in which Jenelle is claiming that she is "getting her life together," all while her current life is playing out online like a white trash telenova.

In a few years, no one will be talking about Jenelle, and I fear that she's in for a rude awakening. It will be very hard for her to adjust to life off-camera and out of the spotlight. I foresee her continuing her hijinks well into the future, just to keep feeding her fame addiction.

Chapter 10

COREY & LEAH: DOOMED TO FAIL?

Corey Simms cried tears of joy as he watched his 18 year-old bride, **Leah Messer**, walk down a makeshift aisle at their October 17, 2010 wedding in Charleston, West Virginia. The romantic affair – staged on a sunny Sunday afternoon at picturesque Coonskin Park – was like a scene plucked from a Hollywood movie. Leah stunned in the satin, ivory-colored **Maggie Sottero** gown her mother purchased for $1549, while Corey paid tribute to his Mountain State roots with a camouflage tie and vest under his black tuxedo jacket.

Watching the newlyweds toast to their future – with Coca-Cola! – and dance to **John Michael Montgomery's** "I Swear," it was almost impossible to imagine that just six months later, they would be tangled in nasty public divorce, with rumors of cheating, lies and physical abuse rocking the *Teen Mom* universe. It was a lethal combination of infidelities, money problems and pressures from becoming overnight celebrities that doomed the proud parents of 15 month-old twins **Aleeah** and **Aliannah** from the moment they said, "I do," Leah's mother **Dawn Spears** says. "Do I think [the show] enabled a bunch of drama issues for these kids? Yes I do," she says. "Drama sells."

Longing For Her Father's Love

Leah may have been young when she married, but Dawn was even younger. She met Leah's father, **Gary**, at her church and after a short courtship, began begging her parents to allow them to marry. They reluctantly agreed, on the condition that the young couple didn't have children for at least two years. But that didn't work out. "I got married at 16 and got pregnant [with Leah] two months later," Dawn says. "So I was 16 and pregnant too – but I was married first!"

As a child, Leah was "wild...but a good kid" -- a lot like her daughter Aleeah, Dawn remembers: "If you watch her story, she is so determined, like nothing's going to stop her from making it. She's been like that since she was little." Leah, one of three children, was in kindergarten when her parents decided to split. She was particularly close with her father – a real "Daddy's girl," Dawn remembers. "But [after the divorce] they didn't have much of a relationship because he would call and promise them stuff for Christmas, or say he was coming to see them, and they'd sit and wait on him and he'd never show up. She'd sit there crying, waiting for him to show up and he'd never come around."

Dawn believes the absence of a consistent father figure in Leah's life may have enticed her to marry at such a young age. "All her life all she wanted was a relationship with her daddy," Dawn says. "She yearned for that. It was a constant letdown for her. I think that's what her thing is, with relationships and men. For some people, it just affects them for the rest of their lives."

Dawn, a dental office associate, remarried just two months after her divorce was finalized and admits Leah was reluctant to accept her new stepdad, **Lee Spears**. "For the longest time they didn't get along because she thought he was trying to replace her daddy," she says. "They did [start getting along] later on, but she gave him a rough road. Her stepdad raised her from kindergarten on."

As a teen, Leah thrived. A popular cheerleader at Herbert Hoover High School, she got good grades and never had a problem making friends. She started dating **Robbie Kidd** around age 13 – a relationship that lasted three years. When the romance fizzled out in early 2009, Leah, a sophomore, hooked up with Corey, a senior at nearby Clay County High School. Leah previously dated one of Corey's good friends, her own best friend, **Amy LaDawn Nichols**, tells us: "After her and that guy split up, she went out with Corey and that's how they ended up together."

One month into their relationship, Leah attended her school's prom – without Corey. He didn't want to attend, but stopped by Leah's house to take pictures before. Later that night, they met up for an unprotected romp in the back of Corey's truck. That's when they have speculated the twins were conceived.

Dawn admits that she knew her daughter was sexually active and did her best to promote birth control. "I had her on the [Depo-Provera] shots," she says. "She missed a month in between getting shots, and that's when she got pregnant."

The day Leah got the news, Dawn was on a business trip about an hour from home. The couple drove to her hotel to break the news. "I always told my children that I don't care what it is, don't hide anything from me," Dawn remembers. "You can come and tell me everything. We've always had a really close relationship."

Robbie Kidd returns from an honest day's work.

Though shocked by Leah's announcement, Dawn says she immediately pledged to support her daughter while others – most notably, Gary – did not. "My dad didn't like the idea at all," Leah told *Entertainment Weekly* in 2010. "He's not really around, but he called me said some pretty harsh things. Things that really hurt. But he's not around so he can't really say much. And my stepdad didn't talk to me for a little while. It was really upsetting to know that I hurt him. I was five months pregnant when we started talking again."

Then came an even bigger bombshell. Dawn says her heart "just dropped" when she learned that Leah was expecting twins. "The nurse looked over and said, 'Honey, I hate to be the bearer of bad news to a 16-year-old girl that's pregnant with twins,'" Dawn remembers. "That's what she said to us." Leah was plagued with health problems during her pregnancy. At 15 weeks, she was put on mandatory bed rest. Her mother moved a bed into the living room of her house, where Leah slept, ate and completed her classwork.

Bumps On The Road To The Altar

Corey and Leah remained together during her pregnancy, but split just weeks after their girls' December 2009 birth. They got back together six months later. Soon, they had moved in together and began talking about getting married. Weddings make for great television, and that fact wasn't lost on the production team that had been trailing Leah for months.

"I don't think MTV *made* them get married, but I definitely think that they pressured them to do it," Amy says. "They really wanted it on the show." According to Amy, the network offered to help the struggling young parents pay for many wedding-related expenses. "I don't think they would have rushed it like they did had it not been for *Teen Mom 2*," she says.

As the big day drew near, some close to Leah began to worry things were moving too fast for the teen. Amy, in fact, admits she was skeptical the relationship would last from the start. "They had a lot going against them — like where they were living and how his family tried to interfere," she says.

Even before they tied the knot, it became clear that the relationship was not as warm and fuzzy as it appeared on TV. Multiple sources have confirmed that after Corey and Leah moved into together, fights and name-calling became frequent. Leah was devastated to discover that her husband-to-be preferred watching adult movies to having sex with her. Soon, the couple's fights turned physically violent, Amy says.

Still, Leah was determined to make things work for the girls and decided to move forward with the wedding – even though she had secretly been texting back and forth with her ex. A week before the big day, Dawn hosted a bachelorette party that lasted well into the night. "I went over to her house after her party died down," Robbie told *OK!* magazine. "Her friends were still there. Leah and I went into her sister **Victoria**'s room. We talked a little and then we slept together." Robbie told the magazine he left Dawn's house at around 2:30 AM, unhappy that Leah still planned to go through with the wedding. Meanwhile, Dawn says she had no idea of what had happened that night – although Corey would later accuse her of knowingly keeping the secret from him.

"Corey said 'You knew about Leah and Robbie [sleeping together] at Leah's bridal shower,'" Dawn recalled of a showdown that was cut from the *Teen Mom 2* reunion special. "I said, 'No I did not until later on.' And he said, 'Yes you did.' Even if I had known, if my daughter came and trusted me, I'm not going to cause trouble for her. I didn't agree with what Leah did, but just like I told her, 'If you fall on your face, I'll be there to pick you up.'

"I was being truthful when I told Corey that I did not know about it, but he just called me a liar, but he has a right to believe whatever he want," Dawn says. "I don't care, people can think what they want about me. But, I don't sit around and tell my daughter that it's OK to go out and mess around with other men."

Amy, who didn't condone Leah's infidelity, does offer her best guess at what went down: "She ended up straying on him before the wedding because he didn't make her feel loved or needed and at the time I think she just got caught up in the moment. At the time, she was just emotionally broken. She wanted a family life and I know she loved Corey, but I don't think their relationship was anywhere near where it needed to be to get married."

Leah later admitted that she knew she was making a mistake by marrying Corey. "I do think we rushed into the marriage quickly," she confessed during a *Teen Mom* 2 after show special. "We just wanted the family, like husband and wife, and the kids. Both of us knew that we shouldn't have got married, because we were both doing things that we shouldn't have been doing at the time."

On their wedding day, Amy – who served as one of Leah's bridesmaids – says the newlyweds were basically at the mercy of the show's producers.

"We didn't have to reenact anything that day, but we had to do a lot of stuff that they wanted us to," she recalls. "They wanted to film everything that we did. They had a lot to do with how everything was planned that day. They pretty much planned it how they wanted it."

Made-For-TV Divorce

The couple's six-month marriage was riddled with fights, according to multiple sources. Corey's disinterest in sex and preoccupation with porn eventually sparked a major, blowout, Amy says. The incident, she explains, took place after a disagreement about the lack of intimacy in their relationship. Leah spent several nights at her mother's house and returned home to find a huge stash of XXX movies on the living room TV. "[Corey] threw a remote through the wall and put his hands around [Leah's] neck because she caught him watching porn after not having sex with her," Amy remembers.

Short tempers were not uncommon in the relationship, Amy says. And she believes there were several times when Corey became violent with his bride-to-be. "I had seen bruises on her neck before that," she says. "She had tried to play it off as a hickey or whatever, but we all knew that wasn't the case."

According to Amy, the final straw came when Corey allegedly hit Leah in the face with an envelope, leaving a gash under her eye. "She was playing with Aleeah while he was on the phone," she remembers. "They were making noise and he told her to shut up. After that, Leah went to stay at her mom's and Dawn was basically like, 'That's it. That's enough.'"

Both Amy and Dawn say the couple spent their brief marriage being constantly hovered over by Corey's family. "His mom [Donna] would always tell her how to raise the kids, how to keep her house and how to run her marriage," Amy says. "Leah got along really well with Corey's dad, **Jeff**, but it was her and Donna that didn't get along."

And, of course, there were money problems. Leah was eager to move out of their beat-up house, but Corey wanted to use the couple's dwindling cash supply to buy a new truck and a four-wheeler. When

Leah found out that Corey was about to use a large chunk of the money that they had earned from the show on new "toys," she was enraged.

Leah and the twins

"I think their failure to communicate properly about what they wanted to do about the money from the show, how the money was going to be spent, that helped lead to the divorce," Amy says.

"Leah's on the show because of her girls. She wanted to use that money to buy a home. Because of the show, they had the financial resources to better their living situation, and Leah felt like all Corey wanted to do was get a four-wheeler so he could go out muddin' and get a nice jacked-up truck. She felt like his priorities just weren't right."

Eventually, Corey began turning his attention to other women – including single teen mother **Amber Scaggs**. The pair hooked up months before Leah officially filed for divorce, Amy says. "Amber had moved from Texas to West Virginia because she has family [there]. I remember in March before Leah filed for divorce, Corey had gone out to Buffalo Wild Wings without Leah. I called Corey because we assumed he was there with Leah but he wasn't. That's when we found out they weren't together and that's the night I guess he met Amber.

"Leah had gotten into his email account, which linked to his *Facebook*, so every time he'd get a *Facebook* message from Amber, Leah would see it," Amy explained.

Producers were forced to edit the story so it looked as if the hookup took place after the divorce. "Corey was cheating just as much (as Leah)," Dawn says. "He wouldn't admit it on camera, so they couldn't present it on the show. They were both cheating. Leah knew about it, but he wouldn't let them film it."

Camera crews did their best to capture the relationship as it crumbled. And what they couldn't get the first time, was carefully recreated, Amy says: "Originally Corey promised if she reenacted the scene where she talks about sleeping with Robbie, and admitted her mistake to the world that he would stay with her. So she agreed and they went back and staged all that. It didn't happen the way it was portrayed on the show. Leah told him face-to- face that she cheated; he didn't hear it through the grapevine like it was shown on the show. That was done just to get the attention of the viewers but all it did was make Leah look absolutely horrible."

Desperate to keep her marriage intact, Leah agreed to let the producers restage the scene where she admitted to cheating. Corey, however, refused to admit his own indiscretions. "[MTV] was like, 'Unless he admits it on camera, we can't put it on the show," Dawn says. "He let [Leah] take the blame when in reality he was just as bad. Leah told me, 'I may be the one that has to go down for this, but I'm going to tell the truth!'"

"In reality, Leah wouldn't have had to say anything publically," Amy says. "She had hoped that they could work it out. She really did try all kinds of things to get him to stay married, counseling and stuff, but he didn't want any of it, which we had figured out later was because he was already seeing Amber. He had flown Amber out and she was staying at her mom's house. Legally they were separated but still married at the time."

Leah's decision to publically admit her infidelities opened her up to public condemnation by many fans of the show.

"After season 2 [aired], she had a lot of emotional problems," Amy says. "She was on depression and anxiety meds. Not only did the divorce affect her negatively, but [doing] the show and reliving it, and the way it all played out, did. As you know they get a lot of footage but you barely see any of it so she had no clue that they were going to edit it in the way that they did.

"The night that it was shown, Leah was absolutely distraught, and pissed off," Amy remembers. "She called MTV and they kept telling them they were sorry, they didn't know, but they told her that she can defend herself publically, but Leah didn't want to do that to Corey."

The backlash from fans, along with the constant exposure of her life, has made Leah sometimes regret the decision she made at 18 to go on *Teen Mom 2*.

"She has told me that she kind of wishes she had never done it," Amy says. "But at the same time she's thankful that she did get it because it has helped tremendously with Ali's medical bills, and it's helped her become a financially stable young woman. But, I don't think she's happy with the way it's all turned out. She never expected it all to end up like this."

Chapter 11

GIRLS BEHAVING BADLY

Deep inside, **Amber Portwood** knew that prison time was the only thing that could save her life. By the time she appeared in front of Madison County Indiana **Judge David Happe** on June 5, 2012, the troubled MTV mom had already made up her mind to abandon a court-ordered rehab program and surrender to five years in the big house.

"In my situation, I felt in the program there were a lot of eyes on me," she told *ABC News* days later. "And it was very uncomfortable. I was not using my anti-psych medication even. I was very depressed, all alone, all bitter at everybody. I felt like that wasn't the life I wanted to live, I felt like I'd rather do my time, and get it over with, and make the best out of the situation that's been handed to me."

Amber, just 22, had been sucked into a downward spiral fueled by anger, loneliness and drug addiction. She escaped serious slammer time in November 2010 after kicking, shoving, slapping and punching **Gary Shirley** – the father of her then one-year-old daughter, **Leah**. But the high school dropout – who struggles with bipolar disorder – was busted again in December 2011 when probation officers discovered a large stash of prescription pills in her home. "She said she was taking the drugs for a medical condition," County Prosecutor **Rodney Cummings** told *The Indianapolis Star*. "But the physician treating her did not support that."

Amber spent a month in the clink before reaching a plea deal that included participation in the drug rehab program. She was making every effort to stay clean, her brother **Shawn** told *OK!* magazine. Doctors even refused to give her over-the-counter painkillers after an emergency gallbladder operation in the spring of 2012. But somehow, Amber found a supply of Suboxone. The drug – which is often prescribed to treat opiate addition – began to deepen her depression. "She started using right after her surgery and then she realized she couldn't stop," Shawn said. Unable to find work and facing her demons amid the glare of a bright media spotlight, a despondent Amber consumed 30 pills in just three days in what she later admitted was a second attempt to end her life.

"The depression took over and I would just take four or five at a time beneath my tongue and nod out," she said. "I felt the same way I felt a couple of years back, when I, you know, tried to commit suicide."

Despite the relapse, Amber would likely have been given additional opportunities to get back on track and avoid being thrown into a population of murderers, rapists and other hardened criminals. "But she just said she couldn't do it and she wanted out of the program," Cummings said. "I don't know that she realized she would actually go to prison... I don't think she's been realistic about the whole thing all along. Whatever celebrity comes along with [being on MTV], I think she thought it was going to prevent her from being held accountable. That just has not been accurate."

Amber could have avoided prison time by completing the rehab program. If she keeps her nose clean, Amber could be eligible for parole in late 2014 – when her daughter, Leah, is six.

In the meantime, Amber told *ABC News* that she plans to "try to better myself for when I get out. I'll be off the drugs. I'll have an education to get me a job. I am not just going to sit. I am going to do substance abuse classes. I am going to get my G.E.D."

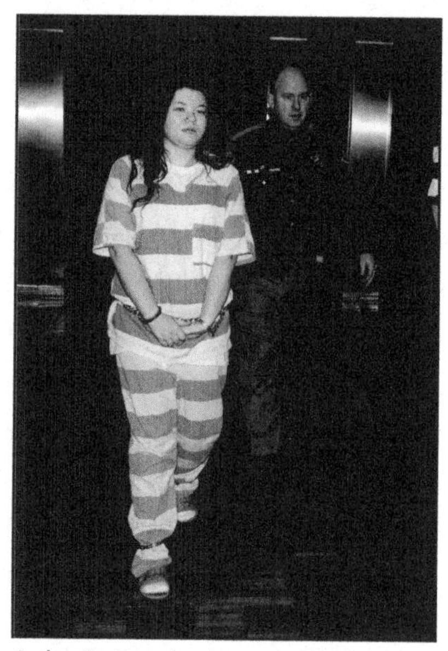

Amber Portwood arrives at Indiana's Madison County Courthouse.

Amber – who signed over full custody of her daughter to Gary in August 2011 – has long blamed MTV and the *Teen Mom* franchise for her problems.

After spending 24 hours in the slammer for attacking Gary in 2010, she told *Life & Style* magazine. "I wouldn't have been in jail because nobody would have known about it." Amber also lamented to *TMZ* cameras: "I might get attention, but it's not the right attention. I don't want to be known as 'Amber from *Teen Mom*.'"

At a December 2011 court hearing, Amber told the judge that she felt "pressured" and "exploited" through her work with MTV. "I want to quit [the show], and I will," she said.

Liz Gateley, an original producer on both *Teen Mom* and *16 and Pregnant* insists the show does everything it can to provide support for its young stars. "We put lots of things in place when we were at MTV to give them access to professional help when they needed it," she says. "But also just to be there and talk to us when they needed to talk to us. My feeling always in those situations and it goes back to every show I have ever done, it comes down to family. How you were raised and the support you had. I don't know that whether we had cameras or not on Amber, that any of that wouldn't have happened in her life."

UPDATE: FEBRUARY 18, 2013

Amber is making great strides in prison, her brother Shawn reported in a personal blog post: "She has had a lot of negative press in the past, which portrayed her as a very hateful individual. And she was for a while. She did not know how to control her anger or even shut up when she needed to. But now I am happy to say that I absolutely believe that it is all behind her now."

Shawn has been corresponding with his sister mostly via email and video chat during her incarceration. During an MTV special in October 2012, Amber said only her mother **Tanya** and **Dr. Drew Pinsky** had come to see her. (Gary has since been to see her as well.)

"After Amber was sent to prison she had a lot to think about and a lot to change about herself," Shawn wrote. "She had to first realize what was important to her, which was her health and most importantly, Leah. I put them in that order because if she were to remain unhealthy then Leah's importance would be non-existent."

Shawn says Amber has been participating in the prison's drug and rehabilitation program. She is also working toward her G.E.D and has completed an anger management program

"That is the one difference that I see in her most," he wrote. "She does not get nearly as angry as she used to. In addition, she nearly never curses, and when she does it is not that vulgar. In a letter Amber sent she said, "I make sure I laugh or smile everyday here. I feel emotions, happiness, anger, and sadness but that is still better than before when all I felt was high." These programs have helped her immensely and changed her thought process, which is something she told me needed to be changed."

Though Amber has grabbed more than her share of headlines in the past four years, she's not the only cast member to run afoul of the law – not by a long shot. Nearly a dozen of the girls (and in some cases their family members) have ended up in police custody.

Who can forget these gems:

DEBRA DANIELSON
Farrah's Mom Gets Abusive
January 16, 2010

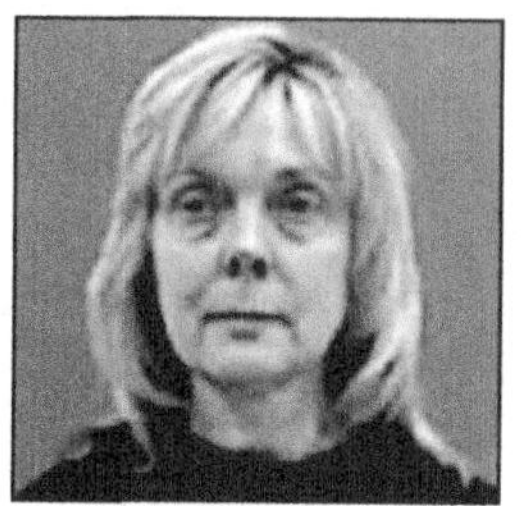

Farrah's mom, Debra, is arrested for assaulting her daughter. Police arrive at Debra's house after receiving reports of a domestic disturbance. (It was later determined that the fight between Debra and Farrah was over the childcare of Farrah's daughter, **Sophia**.) Deb allegedly grabbed Farrah by the throat and struck her on the side of her face and mouth. When the cops arrived, she was reportedly holding a kitchen knife in each hand.

Per the official arrest report:

"On the date of this report, the arrest, Debra Danielsen had been arguing in the home's kitchen with the victim (daughter, Farrah Abraham) over child care issues as well as other problems. The two both live together at [deleted] Willow Avenue. The victim stated that Danielson threw a MTV Tee shirt at her. The shirt landed on near the victim's infant daughter who began to cry.

The victim was yelling at Danielson over the shirt throwing and Danielson grabbed her by the throat. The victim pushed Danielson's hand away from her. Victim stated that Danielson then hit her along the right side of her head and hit her in the mouth. I observed multiple small cuts to the right side of the victim's mouth. Debra Danielsen was arrested for domestic Abuse Serious."

Deb later took a plea deal for the incident, and the aftermath was a key plotline for the second season of *Teen Mom*. Months later, Debra was asked by **Dr. Drew** if she regretted striking her daughter. "No," she replied. "I think that as a parent, if you love your child, you have to tell them when enough is enough on something. You're there to guide them. It doesn't mean you're overbearing as I've been called, but it means that you have to love them."

AUBREY WOLTERS

Banned From Walmart - For Stealing!

May 20, 2010

Aubrey Wolters of *16 and Pregnant* season two gives her 17 month-old son a firsthand look at the criminal justice system – by bringing him along for a shoplifting spree at the Prescott, Arizona Walmart. Aubrey, 17 at the time, was with an unnamed friend when store security allegedly caught her swiping $29.66 worth of eyeliner and makeup brushes.

According to cops, her accomplice had placed the items in her purse. The newly divorced mom landed in even more hot water when police later discovered a stash of drugs – including Ritalin (used to treat ADHD) and Oxycontin in her purse. An official police report says Aubrey didn't have a prescription for either. (Shocker!) Both Aubrey and her pal were charged with shoplifting – and banned from returning to the world's largest retailer for a full year. Aubrey was also slapped with additional charges for possessing drugs without a prescription.

Authorities say she claimed the Oxycontin was her grandmother's and the Ritalin belonged to her ex-husband. **Brandon Akerill** did eventually produce a valid prescription but said he couldn't explain how the pills got into Aubrey's purse. He was given custody of young **Austin** while Aubrey got carted off to juvenile detention.

After the charges became public, Aubrey turned to her *Facebook* fan page to tell her side of the story. Here it is, in all its unedited glory:

"I was never charged with shoplifting (didn't steal anything girl i was with did) & also had a single pill on me which was for my mema & the charge was a yr ago & will be expunged from my record... I went to walmart with a girl I knew & right before entering told her not to steal anything because my husband worked security & walmart had camera operators plus of course I had Austin. She told me it was chill. Then walked through the store a little bit, she wandered off & we eventually met back up. When we walked out the doors i had no idea she'd stolen anything, I didn't even think it was a big deal because I hadn't stolen anything. (Never got a shoplifting charge) When the cop searched my purse i wasn't worried at all because once again I didn't know. I'm not an oxi user & i don't do heroine. If I did I certainly would have hidden it or something because I had plenty of opportunity... The felony will be removed from my record now that I'm 19 yrs. old & have paid my fines. I have a court date set in Arizona. I was ordered to write a paper on the dangers of giving someone a prescription that is not there own & the courts said to come back in a year...

The girl that gave the magazines this info... is the same girl who got me arrested. She's always hated me & thought she could make some easy money by selling this story even though it was a long time ago."

She also had a pretty clever explanation for the drugs that cops found in her purse:

"My mema's prescription ran out. She was in pain, I'd gotten it from a friends mom who had the same prescription. I was not carrying around a bunch of drugs, I had a single pill on me & I'd gotten it 15 mins before hand & was taking it to m...y mema. I didn't even know how

much trouble I could get in for having it otherwise I would have hidden it."

According to *E! News*, the case was closed on June 14, 2010, when Aubrey wrapped up a court-appointed drug diversion program. In a previous run-in with the law, Aubrey had her driver's license suspended for failing to pay a speeding ticket.

VALERIE FAIRMAN

Beats Up Her Mama

April 5, 2011

The *16 and Pregnant* season two alum spent several nights as a guest at the Chester County (Pennsylvania) Youth Center after unleashing a violent assault on the woman who adopted her.

Val – who was being home schooled after disciplinary problems at her local high school – reportedly punched and pushed her mother to the ground, breaking her vertebrae. The high school junior, 17, was charged by state police and taken into custody. After being released from detention, the mother of (then) 19 month-old **Nevaeh** was placed under house arrest until her hearing.

JENNIFER DEL RIO v. JOSH SMITH

Who Punched Who?

April 18, 2011

Cops in Hillsborough County, Florida are called to the home of 19-year-old **Josh Smith** – after he claimed to be pummeled by the hot-tempered mother of his twins! Smith – who was arrested on November

4, 2010 and ordered to complete a domestic violence program after allegedly attacking **Jennifer Del Rio** – says the 17 year-old mom opened up a can of whoop ass when he tried to end their relationship.

According to police reports, Jennifer became "irate" and "punched him in the face and pulled on his shirt." He eventually pushed her away as an act of self-defense. When no arrest was made, Jennifer quickly took to her official *Facebook* fan page, and claimed "Josh lied to the cops... He punched himself and ripped his shirt... He lied under oath & that will be proved." The way she tells it, their latest dispute began when she drove Josh home from a job interview. He requested to keep one of the children overnight and she objected.

That's when Jennifer says Josh pushed her into a fence and then disappeared inside the house – returning a few minutes later with a ripped shirt and bloody nose. She later told *TMZ* that Josh called the cops because it was "her turn to go to jail" – "payback," she says, for an explosive incident months earlier when she had him arrested. In March 2011, Jennifer filed a restraining order against her long-ago love, claiming he had been "harassing and threatening" her and "saying he will have [her] raped." Josh "has attempted to kidnap [the] children," she claimed, adding that "due to [his] violence [she] is frightened for her life and children's life."

APRIL PURVIS

Whitney's Mom Caught With Crystal Meth

June 5, 2011

Whitney Purvis' mom enjoyed her own 15 minutes of fame after being popped for possession of meth and marijuana. April, 37, was pulled over by police near her home in Rome, Georgia, during a random road check.

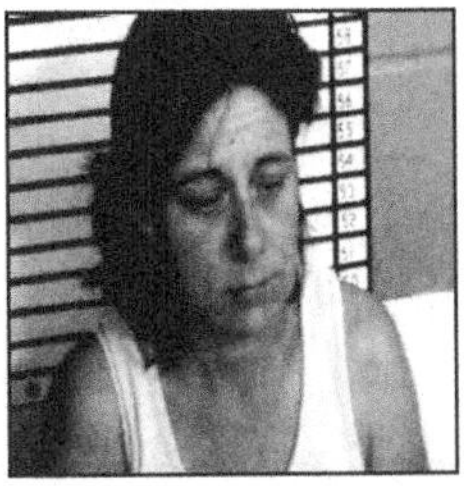

According to *The Rome News Tribune*:

"The officer noted that Purvis smelled of marijuana and, after a K9 search of her vehicle, the officer found marijuana between the driver's and passenger seat of the car. Upon further inspection, suspected meth was found in the pocketbook of Purvis. Purvis is charged with felony possession of methamphetamines and misdemeanor possession of less than one ounce marijuana. Victor Lamar Clement, 48...was also arrested. He is charged with misdemeanor possession of less than one ounce of marijuana. Neither party arrested admitted to whether the pot was theirs."

After the arrest, Whitney told *TMZ*: "What my mom does, does not effect me. I'm nothing like [my] parents. I do not want my son to grow up how I did." April was featured prominently in Whitney's episode of *16 and Pregnant,* as both mother and daughter were expecting at the same time.

CLEONDRA CARTER

Cops Called After Domestic Disturbance

August 28, 2011

Cleondra (of *16 and Pregnant* season three) and her normally even-tempered baby daddy, **Mario Escovedo**, spent the night in separate cinderblock cells after cops responded to a loud domestic disturbance at their Horn Lake, Mississippi home.

"Mario and I are still together," Cleondra revealed in an interview just weeks before the double arrest. "It was rocky but we just had to figure out how to juggle each other and Kylee with us both working full-time jobs, but we're good now." According to *The Desoto Times Tribune*, both were charged with domestic assault and released on bail (his, $1,000; hers, $500). "Mario and I did not press charges against each other," she says. "So we just had to pay court fines. It did not go on our permanent records."

KIANNA RANDALL

Locked Up After Botched Robbery

August 28, 2011

Some people just aren't cut out for a life of crime! 18 year-old **Kianna Randall** and her underage fiancé, **Zak Hegab**, both landed in the clink (along with five other knuckleheads) after a botched robbery attempt at an elderly woman's house in Texas. Apparently no one seemed to notice that the lady was home!

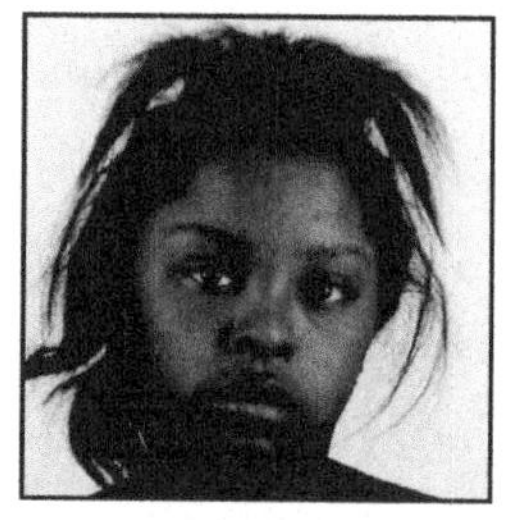

To make matters worse, Zak – who was just 16 at the time – was caught with a loaded 9mm in his pants. Kianna, from *16 and Pregnant* season three, was charged with two counts of burglary and eventually sprung free on a $40,000 bond. She ended up getting ten years probation but returned to jail in Tarrant County, Texas on December 14, 2012 on a violation that county officials say "stemmed from the original arrest." Kianna was released on March 27, 2013 and immediately began posting half-naked photos of herself on *Instagram* along with the message "Free My Husband." Zak is expected to be a guest of the Lone Star State Department of Corrections until 2027. In the meantime, Zak's mom has been helping out with baby **Kay'den**.

WHITNEY PURVIS

Steals Pregnancy Tests From Walmart

March 1, 2012

Whitney was detained in a Georgia Walmart for applying the five finger discount to a First Response pregnancy test – and using it in the store! The 20-year-old first time offender stashed the $15.98 kit in a hooded jacket, according to police reports, then "took it to the restroom with her." She was busted by store security and placed under citizen's arrest after trying to sneak out of a side door. "My boyfriend was with me and he had money – but I didn't want to freak him out," she later revealed. "I was just being stupid with my decisions. I wish I would have handled the situation better."

Whitney received a free ride to the nearby police station where she was booked for misdemeanor theft and shoplifting. The pregnancy test turned up negative, which was good news for the cash-strapped single mom. "I was excited because I didn't want another kid," she said. "I already have one."

The results of Whitney's legal drama were also quite positive. "My charges are officially dropped!" she wrote on *Facebook* on March 16, 2012. "Whoop, whoop, thank you baby Jesus." [sic]

Whitney's celebration was short-lived, however. In December 2012, she was arrested again, alongside her baby-daddy, **Weston Gosa**, on a charge of criminal trespassing. *TMZ* reported that warrants were issued for Weston and Whitney's arrests after they allegedly smashed someone's cell phone and laptop.

DANIELLE CUNNINGHAM
Charged With Assaulting Grandmother
July 7, 2012

The girl who once dreamed of becoming an attorney ended up needing one herself, when she was arrested after getting into a physical fight with her grandmother. Four months after pleading guilty to an unrelated assault charge, Danielle, who appeared on the third season of *16 and Pregnant)* offered this explanation: "My grandma isn't some frail old lady, she's only 53... She locked me and Jamie Jr. out of the house in 100-degree weather so I started freaking out, pounding on the door as I had a right to. She ended up throwing my purse in my face and saying I'll never be nothing. She pushed me into a bedroom so I pushed her out. She freaked out and called the cops. And I got to go to jail." Danielle pled not guilty to the charge of disorderly conduct. She was released two days later and ordered to stay away from her grandmother. The charges were later downgraded and she received one year of probation for her crimes.

FARRAH ABRAHAM
Arrested For D.U.I.
March 18, 2013

Farrah didn't exactly have the luck of the Irish when she was pulled over on her way home from a St. Patrick's Day celebration in Omaha, Nebraska. What might have been a routine celebrity D.U.I. escalated into an embarrassing public relations nightmare, as Farrah took to *Twitter* and the tabloids insisting she did nothing wrong.

"It's Amazing what people believe & makeup (LOVE MY LIFE) #Thank #God #I'mSuccessful & I don't care about drama! #HaveAGreatDay." she tweeted before telling her side of the warped story to *In Touch* magazine: "I was out with my sister. I did not plan to drink because I was sick, so I took the role of being in charge and making sure my sister and I would return home together and safely," she explained. "At 10 p.m., I tried to leave, and at that time, my sister was not ready to leave, so I had been sipping on drinks to pass the time."

What Farrah failed to mention was that when she went to retrieve her car, she nearly crashed into a police cruiser! The official police report says the belligerent reality star intentionally bit the Breathalyzer device to prevent it from functioning properly and repeatedly banged her head against the window of the squad car she was placed in.

"My hands were, like, behind my back and I play soccer so I'm like, 'Well, if I can't use my hands, I have to use my head,'" she told *TMZ*. "I was clearly trying to get the attention of the police officer who was talking to my friend at the time...I was wondering, why are they not talking to me?"

And that .147 she blew, which was almost twice the legal limit?

"Because I'm sick, I could not give an accurate Breathalyzer test, due to coughing and shortage of breath," she says. "I have a lawyer and all will work out with my ticket."

Naturally, not many people bought Farrah's story. One person close to her told *Today.com*: "She can say what she wants, but the truth is that her sister Ashley and her friends were miles away by the time Farrah got arrested," said the source, who noted that several local businesses were sponsoring free cab rides home in the area. "A friend of Farrah's offered to give her a ride home before they left, but Farrah didn't take it."

Chapter 12

BAD BOYS AND BABY DADDIES

Courtland Rogers – the former roofer and childhood friend who took **Jenelle Evans** as his bride in December 2012 – just couldn't ring in the new year without lobbing one last zinger at her trouble-prone ex. "Just leave me and my WIFE ... Mrs. Rogers alone," he tweeted to **Kieffer Delp** during Christmas week, implying – in a not so subtle way – that Jenelle nearly died after he introduced her to hardcore drugs.

"Wait till they see this next season on how u did jenelle and got her hooked on heroin ... she almost died cuz of u dumbass," Courtland wrote. "U got jenelle strung out and then u bailed on her when she needed u most! And everyone thinks u are the good guy! This is sad." [sic]

Kieffer is no stranger to drama – especially when Jenelle is in the mix. One of three sons born to **Vickie Delp-Ham** of Carney's Point,

New Jersey, he essentially drifted from couch to couch before hooking up with the young mom at a party in 2010. Their sometimes toxic relationship drove a wedge between Jenelle and her mom, **Barbara**, after the teen troublemakers swiped her credit cards and took off for a weekend of pot-fueled hijinks during the first season on *Teen Mom 2*.

After countless breakups, makeups and run-ins with the law, Kieffer and Jenelle eventually turned on each other. In 2012, Kieffer leaked nude photos of Jenelle on the web and threatened to release a homemade sex tape. Jenelle, meanwhile, sold his woodworking tools to a pawn shop, and in throwing what may be the most shocking punch, appeared to reveal Kieffer's biggest secret to her more than 700,000 followers on *Twitter*. "Ask Kieffer where his son is," she posted in October. His online response: "I'm not talking about my son on *Twitter*."

As of March 2013, Kieffer was living back in New Jersey, and dating single mom **Tabatha Shaw**. He continues to tweet freely, even getting in a jab at Courtland when Jenelle appeared to go AWOL in the middle of the night: "She used to do that to me too," he wrote, "sucks to have a sh*tty disloyal gf #usedtofeelyurpain."

KEIFFER'S RAP SHEET

October 15, 2010: Jenelle and Kieffer are popped for breaking and entering, possession of marijuana and possession of drug paraphernalia. Kieffer's charges are eventually dropped, while Jenelle gets probation for the possession charges.

June 16, 2011: Kieffer lands in police custody (again) after punching out one of Jenelle's former pals – and her male companion – in a fracas outside a North Carolina convenience store. According to the official police report, Kieffer left the unlucky dude "bleeding heavily" from the smack down. The hoodie-sporting bad boy quickly fled the scene but turned himself in a week later. He was charged with simple assault and assault on a female. Jenelle, meanwhile, took to *Facebook* to clear his name. "He didn't touch that girl," she wrote. "[but she] was the crazy fan who attacked me."

August 30, 2011: Kieffer is arrested in Baltimore on five different misdemeanor drug charges. All totaled, he faces a possible 12 years in prison and $77,000 in fines, per the Maryland State Commission on Criminal Sentencing Policy, but ends up getting released from Anne Arundel Correction Detention Center on November 1.

November 12, 2011: Oak Island (North Carolina) Police transport Kieffer to the Brunswick County Jail. The charge this time: seven failures to appear in court. "Mr. Kieffer Delp called the police department and wished to turn himself in for a warrant he was aware of," the arresting officer wrote in his official report. "Mr. Delp met me in the driveway [and] was polite and cooperative."

March 31, 2012: Kieffer proves once again that he has an appetite – for trouble! In one of the juiciest *Teen Mom* arrests yet, he is caught red-handed trying to swipe a prime pair of steaks from a Food Lion supermarket in Oak Island. *RadarOnline* reports that Kieffer was issued a citation – which he refused to sign – and was required to appear in court the following month.

October 4, 2012: A night of partying eventually turns sour when the serial lawbreaker is pulled over for running a stop sign. New Jersey cops find an open container of alcohol in the passenger seat and discover that Kieffer was driving on a revoked license. He is promptly hauled to the Brunswick County Jail. "Showering the county smell off for the LAST time," he tweeted the following afternoon. Jenelle, happy to rub salt in the wound, shared the news of her ex-boyfriend's arrest on *Facebook*:

"Well this just adds to the charges on his record as a felon and adds to the warrants that he has in North Carolina which is a count of three! He also missed his court date pressing charges on my mom and stepdad and missed another court date for a driving while license suspended charge! Wowww, never seen a man in so much trouble!"

ADAM LIND

He fought the law and the law won! **Adam Lind** – the baddest of all *Teen Mom* baby daddies – was sentenced to 180 days in Minnehaha County (South Dakota) jail on March 27, 2013 after pleading guilty to his third drunk driving charge in a year. The father of **Chelsea**'s adorable daughter, **Aubree Skye,** has been behind bars five times since 2010 and racked up more legal problems than anyone else in the show's history.

Adam's fate could actually have been much worse. He was also given two years in the State Penitentiary, with the entire time suspended. 60 days of this sentence – to be served in the Minnehaha County Jail – were also suspended. With credit for two days served he will only be on the hook for 118 days. Adam will also be allowed to leave the lockup for work.

"I got all those DUIs after I turned 21," he revealed at a sentencing for another drunk driving charge just two weeks earlier. "It was just a little fling. I thought I could drive and get away with it. I just kept doing it. Now I realize I can't do it anymore. It's got to stop."

The hammer could not have come down on Adam at a worse time. During a last ditch attempt to keep his client out of the slammer days earlier, public defender **Daniel Haggar** confirmed for the first time in open court that Adam and girlfriend **Taylor Halbur** are expecting a baby together in August 2013.

"He has a three year-old daughter. He has child support obligations for her. He is caught up, so I think that is to his credit," Haggar said, confirming that Adam, 22, has been working part time for his father's dry wall business for close to a year. "We see a lot of people who don't take that responsibility seriously. He has and he does. He intends on keeping that current. He also has another child on the way in August so he is feeling pressure on both sides and I think that it is adding up."

But so were Adam's legal problems. Since 2010, he has been to jail six times and racked up more infractions than anyone else in *Teen Mom* history. Many of his arrests have involved driving without a license or insurance.

Once a star baseball player, Adam was a senior at West Central High School when Chelsea, a junior, discovered she was pregnant in early 2009. Shortly after Aubree's birth, Adam, who seemed to prefer building muscle cars to being a father, became public enemy number one to many viewers for calling his daughter "a mistake" in a nasty text message shown on Chelsea's episode of *16 and Pregnant*. He later admitted to cheating on Chelsea at least five times. The on-off couple got into a heated war on *Facebook* in early 2010, with Chelsea posting "any boy can make a baby but it takes a MAN to be a daddy" and Adam responding, "takes a girl to have a baby and take care of it but it takes a WOMEN to treat her man good and not be a complete f***ing PHSYCO!" [sic]

His parents, Vern and Donna, have done their best to distance themselves from the drama, refusing to appear on camera for either *16 and Pregnant* or *Teen Mom 2*. On the rare occasions they are caught on screen in the background, producers are contractually obligated to blur their faces and bleep out their names. But the Lind's haven't been able to keep their son out of legal trouble.

While Adam's March D.U.I. arrests made national headlines, he managed to keep 25 other legal infractions – from obstruction of an officer to burglary and possession of artificial night vision – well hidden. Until now. We contacted the South Dakota Unified Judicial System and found out more. Here, in chronological order, is a list of Adam's run-ins with the law beginning in mid-2007.

1. **Reckless Driving (Offense Date: 05/31/07)**

   10/03/07: Pled guilty. Sentenced to 20 days in jail, but all 20 days are suspended. Required to pay fines and fees of $544.00

2. **Failure to Renew Vehicle Registration (10/23/07)**

   11/06/07: Didn't show up for his scheduled court date.

   11/09/07: A bench warrant is issued for his arrest after he failed to show in court.

   11/16/07: Pled guilty. Paid fines and fees of $114.00

3. **Speeding (06/18/08)**

   Adam was clocked going 89 mph in a 55 mph zone just after 2:00 AM. That violated the terms of his previous Exhibition Driving run-in from 2007.

   07/02/08: Did not show for his scheduled court date.

   08/06/08: Pled guilty. License suspended. Paid fines and fees of $204.00.

4. **Driving Without a Motorcycle License / Driving Without Eye Protection (02/14/09)**

   03/02/09: Failed to appear for his scheduled court date.

   03/10/09: Pled guilty to both charges. Paid fines and court fees of $124.00.

5. **Speeding (05/04/09)**

Adam was raising hell on his motorcycle once again.

05/14/09: Pled guilty. Paid fines of $110.00.

6. **Failure to Maintain Financial Responsibility - Insurance (06/01/09)**

06/15/09: Failed to appear for scheduled court date.

06/19/09: A bench warrant is issued for his arrest

06/22/09: Charge is dismissed.

7. **Failure to Report an Accident to Police (07/01/09)**

Adam got into a car accident and didn't bother to tell police.

07/24/09: No plea entered. Charge dismissed.

8. **Possession of Alcohol by a Minor (07/11/09)**

07/24/09: Pled guilty. Charge dismissed.

9. **Possession of Alcohol by a Minor (08/16/09)**

A month after skating through his first alcohol-related offense, 18-year-old Adam was once again caught with booze.

08/31/09: Pled guilty. Sentenced to 15 days in jail. License suspended 60 days. Ordered to pay $150 in court fines and fees.

All 15 days are suspended provided there are no similar offenses for one year.

10/15/09: After violating the terms of his suspension, a bench warrant was issued for his arrest.

This time he had his license suspended for 60 days and was sentenced to 15 days in jail; however he did not spend time behind bars, on the condition that he did not reoffend for one year.

10. **Making Unreasonable Noise (09/08/09)**

09/22/09: Didn't show up for scheduled court date

09/28/09: A bench warrant is issued for his arrest

10/15/09: Pled guilty and paid fines

11. **Driving on a Restricted License (09/10/09)**

Just three days after his daughter Aubree's birth, Adam ran afoul of the law again, this time after getting caught driving while his license was restricted.

09/30/09: Failed to show up for schedule court date

10/07/09: A bench warrant is issued for his arrest

12/17/09: Pled guilty. Paid fines and fees of $105.00

12. **Driving Without a License (11/03/09)**

11/07/09: Pled not guilty.

12/17/09: Changed plea to guilty. Paid fines and court fees.

13. **Possession of Alcohol by a Minor / Obstruction of an Officer (05/08/10)**

5/26/10: Pled not guilty to alcohol charge. (It was later dismissed.)

06/09/10: Pled guilty to obstruction charge. Sentenced to 30 days in jail.

Adam's 30 days in lockup were suspended, provided he pay court fees and not have any similar offenses for two years.

14. **Careless Driving/ Failure to Maintain Financial Responsibility-Insurance (08/17/10)**

08/31/10: Pled guilty to both crimes. Sentenced to 10 days in jail.

Once again, Adam served no time behind bars. His sentence was suspended provided he didn't drive without insurance for at least one year and paid all his court-related fines and fees. His drivers license was (again) suspended for 30 days – this time without a work permit.

15. **Failure to Maintain Financial Responsibility (09/05/10)**

10/14/10: Pled guilty. Sentenced to 15 days in jail. Driver's license suspended 30 days.

Adam's entire sentence was suspended provided he didn't drive without insurance for two years.

16. 2nd Degree Burglary / 2nd Degree Petty Theft / Entering or Refusing to Leave/ Failure to Stop for Law Enforcement / Hunting Without a License / Possessing Artificial Night Vision (11/05/10)

11/23/10: Pled guilty to hunting charge. His hunting license was suspended for one year.

01/14/11: Pled not guilty to the Burglary charge. (It was eventually reduced.) Petty Theft charge was dismissed.

02/01/11: Pled guilty to Entering or Refusing to Leave charge. Sentenced to 90 days in jail. Pled guilty to Possessing Artificial Night Vision and had his hunting license revoked for one year. Pled guilty to Failure to Stop for Law Enforcement charge. Sentenced to an additional 30 days in jail.

Adam ended up serving seven days in the slammer, on the condition that he didn't have any trespassing or theft charges for two years. He spent three additional days in jail for his Failure to Stop for Law Enforcement offense.

17. Possession of Alcohol by a Minor (05/07/11)

For the third time in less than two years, Adam was caught with alcohol. This time, the courts weren't as lenient.

08/08/11: Pled guilty.

09/08/11: Driver's license suspended for 30 days. Sentenced to 30 days in jail.

Adam only ended up serving five days of the sentence before being released. He was, however, allowed to leave the jail to go to work.

18. Driving Without a Motorcycle License / Speeding / Driving Without Proper Plates (06/05/11)

06/21/11: Pled guilty to Driving without a Motorcycle License and Speeding charges. Paid fines and fees of $239.00. Driving without Proper Plates charge was dismissed.

08/08/11: A bench warrant is issued for his arrest after he fails to pay his court fees.

19. Resisting Arrest / Disorderly Conduct / Possession of Alcohol by a Minor (07/24/11)

09/08/11: Possession of Alcohol by a Minor charge is dismissed.

11/23/11: Pled guilty to Disorderly Conduct. Sentenced to 30 days in jail.

Adam's entire jail sentence was suspended, provided he didn't rack up any more like offenses for two years.

20. Speeding / Driving with Suspended License (10/06/11)

11/09/11: Pled guilty to both charges. Sentenced to 30 days in jail.

Adam ended up serving only 15 days behind bars. He reported to jail on November 25, 2011 – just a few weeks before the second season of Teen Mom 2 premiered.

21. Driving with Suspended License (12/22/11)

03/21/12: Pled guilty. Sentenced to 30 days in jail. Ordered to pay $176.00 in court costs and attorney fees.

He reported to jail on April 13, 2012 but only ended up serving two days.

22. Driving Under the Influence / Driving with Suspended License / Failure to Maintain Financial Responsibility (01/15/12)

03/6/12: Pled not guilty to Driving on a Suspended License and Failure to Maintain Financial Responsibility (insurance).

06/26/12: Bench warrant issued when Adam fails to appear in court.

08/20/12: Pled guilty to DUI. Scheduled jury trial cancelled.

02/26/13: Sentenced to 30 days in jail.

All 30 days of Adam's sentence were suspended on the condition that he not incur any similar offenses for one year. He was required to pay fines, court costs and attorney fees of $794.00 by August 26, 2013.

23. Driving Under the Influence – 2nd Offense / Driving with Suspended License / Exhibition Driving (03/31/12)

05/31/12: Exhibition Driving charge dismissed.

06/12/12: Pled not guilty to Driving on Suspended License charge.

08/20/12: Pled guilty to DUI charge.

02/26/13: Sentenced to 180 days in jail for DUI charge. Required to pay $559.00 in fines and court costs plus $115.00 in attorney fees. Driver's license revoked for one year.

100 days of Adam's jail term were suspended on the condition he have no major driving violations for one year.

24. Speeding / Driving with Suspended License / Failure to Maintain Financial Responsibility (05/11/12)

05/17/11: Failure to Maintain Financial Responsibility is dismissed.

05/25/11: Plead guilty to Driving with Suspended License and Speeding.

25. Driving with Suspended License / Failure to Maintain Financial Responsibility - Insurance / No Proper License Plates (05/23/12)

06/08/12: Pled not guilty to all charges.

02/26/13: Pled guilty to Driving with Suspended License charge. Sentenced to 30 days in jail. Driver's license revoked for 30 days. Required to pay $80 in attorney fees.

Received a suspended 20 day sentence but was required to report to Minnehaha County Jail on Sunday, March 17 to serve remaining 10 days, with work release permitted.

26. Driving Without a License (06/29/12)

07/13/12: Pled guilty. Paid fines and court costs.

26. Failure to Appear in Court (07/17/12)

06/28/12: A bench warrant is issued for his arrest.

07/18/12: Posted his own bond.

08/20/12: Pled guilty.

02/26/12: Sentenced to 30 days in jail. Required to pay $80 in attorney fees, but no court costs or fines.

All 30 days of his incarceration were suspended on condition there are no like offenses for two years.

27. Driving With Suspended License / Failure to Maintain Financial Responsibility-Insurance / Failure to Renew Registration (09/22/12)

10/05/12: Failed to appear in court.

11/29/12: Failed to appear in court again.

12/03/12: A bench warrant is issued for failing to appear in court.

01/02/13: Pled not guilty to all crimes

28. Charged with Driving Under Influence- 3rd Offense / Driving With Suspended License/ Failure to Maintain Financial Responsibility / Careless Driving / Making an Illegal Lane Change (11/29/12)

11/29/12: Illegal Lane Change and Careless Driving charges dismissed.

12/13/11: Pled not guilty to D.U.I and Driving with Suspended License charges.

03/11/13: Pled guilty to D.U.I. charge.

Sentenced to 180 days in jail, 60 days suspended

CHARLES ANDREW LEWIS

Jenelle Evans pretty much summed up her feelings about baby daddy **Charles Andrew Lewis** in one heartfelt tweet from January 2011: "Did I mention how much I hate jace's father ?! GET A F—ING LIFEEEEEEEEEEEE."

Andrew – who claims he once worked as a fashion model in New York City – was with the wild teen mom for three years before she became pregnant in late 2008. As he tells it, the first time they met, he walked right up and kissed her. But the young couple was eventually torn apart by Jenelle's infidelity. Though Andrew's name is on Jace's birth certificate, his paternity was in doubt when Jenelle admitted she slept with her friend **Stephen Fullwood** around the same time her baby was conceived. A paternity test in late 2011 confirmed Andrew was, in fact, the boy's father. But by then, the feud was already in high gear.

On December 29, 2010 Jenelle and her mother, Barbara, had Andrew picked up by the Randolph County (North Carolina) Sheriff's Department and placed into custody for 17 days for failing to pay $2,079.67 in child support. He was released on January 14 and required by the court to make monthly payments of $356.00.

A few weeks later, Andrew came out swinging in a bombshell interview with *In Touch* magazine. "I saw [Jenelle] smoking weed when she was three months pregnant," he revealed. "Another time, I found speed in her jacket pocket! I tried to make Jenelle understand how bad it was for the baby, but she didn't care. It completely broke my heart. Isn't that disturbing and disgusting? She had no regard for the safety of her unborn child!"

Though Andrew was present for Jace's birth in August 2009, he left shortly after and had no contact with his son until Jenelle approved a Skype session on Christmas Eve 2011. Within a year, Jenelle claimed he had again fallen behind on child support obligations – this time by

$7,000. He refused to pay because Jenelle and her mother, Barbara, would not let him see or spend time with the boy.

"I love him and I want him in my life," Andrew told *In Touch*. "Jenelle has put me through hell, never letting me see our son." He also said Jenelle "went completely off the deep end" when she learned about his new son, Jacob Michael (b. September 6, 2010), with former girlfriend, **Ashley Termini**. "She was incredibly mean and said I don't deserve to have kids."

Jenelle fired back at her ex in a December 2012 interview with *Wetpaint.com*. "I've tried getting a hold of him, but supposedly he lives in Florida and has a new girlfriend and takes care of his girlfriend's baby, and other than that I don't know about Andrew," she said. "He hasn't come to see Jace or anything."

We reached out to Andrew for an interview and received the following response, which he later posted to Facebook:

> *"I do not want anything to do with (*Teen Mom*) or* 16 and Pregnant, *that's why you never see me on there. It is degrading, and makes teenagers around the world think it is OK to be young mothers creating this baby boom. Knowing that teenage pregnancy is part of one of the top economical downfalls, [MTV] still intend[s] to promote it, on top of that the media and show itself downgrades the person making the entire world believe that one person is bad, etc.*
>
> *They don't care much about you, just the ratings and MTV has a heavy hand at editing drama, drama, drama. You do not see me on that show for a reason and that reason is that once you're off that show that's it for you; no more career moves there. You're gonna be stuck known as a teen mom forever. I respect the business, I've worked in it since I was 17, and if I wanted to become famous or more likely "publicly known" Ii would work a hell of a lot harder*

than just being on a reality TV series which is one of the most lowest ranking spots you can even think of doing in the business. You get no respect from others who worked hard for what they accomplished.

[MTV] takes advantage of teenagers because they want to be on TV, paying them little because the teens do not know the business etiquette. For example, they got like $60,000 a year from what people tell me and when they filmed me for I got $5,000 for every 8 hours of filming that is triple the amount they would get paid annually if they knew how to handle the high tides.

I am in college; I go to Florida State working on my MFA major in film industry. People say I am a drunk loser deadbeat but I am not. I do not drink nor do drugs. I work hard as a full-time student completing my goals I have set in my life.

In conclusion always know what you're getting into. Do your research, learn more. Never jump into things like these teens did, because to me it is not worth it. I've never seen an episode and could care less to do so. I am happy with my life and I have no feeling of how Jenelle went downhill after breaking up with me. She is an adult and she is old enough to make her own decisions and doing that show. When I dated her she was never in trouble with cops, didn't do drugs as [far as] I knew of etc. I kept her boundaries in line.

There you have it.

JO RIVERA

He gave **Kail** a son and – according to her – an STD!

Jo's baby mama shocked even the most in-the-know *Teen Mom 2* fans when she accused the aspiring rapper of infecting her with chlamydia during the season two reunion special in 2011. "I had no idea they were going to bring that up," Jo revealed during a radio interview a year later. "I didn't have any [STDs] so I don't know...."

Kail and Jo have had a contentious relationship at best since they first appeared together on season two of *16 and Pregnant*. Though his parents, **Janet** and **Eddie**, opened up their four bedroom, 3,761-square-foot Easton, Pennsylvania home to Kail when she became pregnant in 2009, Jo was not always thrilled to have his new roommate around. Shortly before the birth of their son, Isaac, the Puerto Rican bad boy cheated on Kail, perhaps squashing any chance of them succeeding as a family.

By 2011, Jo had found a new woman and a new career. He met 21 year-old aspiring model **Vee Torres** when she co-starred in a sexy music video for his first rap single, "Unthinkable." (Jo followed up with another tune, fittingly called "Life As A Teen Father.") By early 2012, he struggled to even remember what attracted him to Kail. "It's hard to say," he told the hosts of North Carolina's "Murphy In The Morning" radio show. "We were young and were attracted to each other. She's not a bad person. We all have our moments."

Jo's Legal Woes

March 27, 2011: Jo gets a face full of law enforcement when he is popped in Warren County, Pennsylvania for being stoned! Jo was riding shotgun in his brother Edward's car when cops spotted sparks shooting out from the undercarriage. They pulled the vehicle over and discovered both siblings were under the influence of marijuana. **Edward** (a/k/a "Junior") was charged with D.U.I., being under the influence of marijuana, driving with a suspended license, and driving an unsafe vehicle, according to the official police report.

JOSHUA DRUMMONDS

Nikkole Paulun describes **Joshua Drummonds** – the often belligerent and disrespectful father of her young son, Lyle – as "a drug addict," who once lived in a "crack house" and broke up with her for refusing to have an abortion. The pair, featured on season two of *16 and Pregnant*, has one of the show's most unhealthy relationships. He stood her up at the homecoming dance, started a fight with her mother, **Rikki**, moments before Lyle's birth, and admitted to cheating on the former cheerleader multiple times.

Josh – who was expelled from high school (but later earned his G.E.D.) – also has a laundry list of legal problems. In May 2011, he racked up three felonies after helping himself to his own mother's checkbook. Over the course of several months, Josh wrote himself five checks ranging from $30-100, for a grand total of $270. When his mom got wind of the diminishing balance, she promptly had him arrested. He later pled guilty to two counts of forgery and one count of larceny, and was sentenced to a year in jail. Josh was released in March 2012 and transferred to a rehab center – which he promptly fled. He was caught using drugs a week later and was sent back to jail until mid-April 2012. Josh quickly became a regular at the Monroe County Jail, having served time in there in 2009 for failing drug tests while in court-mandated rehab, and again in 2010 after Nikkole called the cops on him, knowing that he had outstanding warrants.

The couple first got together when Nikkole was just 15. Despite numerous breakups, they became engaged in late September 2012 – only to end things for good two months later when Nikkole confessed she had been unfaithful. "I've OFFICIALLY moved back to my moms after a NASTY break up with Josh," she posted on *Sulia*. "He caught me cheating & we ... fought and fought and fought. I know he posted a bunch of stuff about us getting back together possibly but I told him my heart was just not in it. I will always care about Josh considering he's been such a big part of my life but as for now I am not capable of loving him and being in a relationship with him. I think we're best off as just friends and co-parenting."

Nikkole, who enrolled at a Toledo, Ohio college after her son's birth, shared several intimate – and disturbing – details about her relationship with Josh in a 2011 posting on Tumblr. They include:

"Josh was in juvy right after I first met him. Why? He had marijuana on him at school & also got in trouble for being on private property. When we started "talking" he had just got out. We started dating a few months later. When we were first dating, he was a homebody. He always sat at home and read or played Wii or whatever. He also loved to cook."

"When I wouldn't abort the baby, Josh changed dramatically. He broke up with me, stopped going to school, and got kicked out of his house. I was dumbfounded by it all. He was literally living in a crack house. I went there once and it was absolutely disgusting. No electricity, holes in the wall, and drugs everywhere. I couldn't believe the person I loved was like this. I tried so hard to save him but I didn't know what to do. I was only 15."

"One night he came in real late and didn't know I was still up. I heard him fiddle with the heat vent for a few minutes. Then he went to bed. When he was taking a shower the next morning I looked in the vent and found two needles. I was beyond shocked. I immediately disposed of them so he couldn't find them. I didn't say a word. I was sitting on the couch later in the day and I heard him go into the room. He came out looking pretty upset and asked me if Lyle had been near the vent. I went into his room with him and confronted him about it. He told me and said he was sorry but nothing could stop him now. He said he wanted help but not to say anything to anyone. So I didn't."

"Finally, on New Year's Eve, he called me and asked me to steal his dad's gun or else he'd shoot up bleach. I decided it was time to tell his mom. She started crying, and me and his sister hurriedly drove to where he was. We found him safe and sound and he ended up coming home with us. About 30 mins after coming home he began to have crazy withdrawals. I didn't know what to do. He was puking and shaking and freaking out. We called an ambulance and the police ended up showing up too since he had warrants we didn't know about.

"He served his time in jail, and when he got out, he went right back at it. I was done. I wasn't letting myself live this life anymore. I decided to call my mom and come home, and of course she said yes. I had all my stuff packed and Lyle in the car, and Josh told me he was going to kill himself. I laughed and said shut up. He held his hand out and in it was a fist full of sleeping pills. He threw them all in his mouth and swallowed. I screamed for his mom to take him to the hospital. I went home after that. I guess he had his stomach

pumped and had to stay for 3 days because he was on suicide watch. I never wanted to be with him again."

On January 23, 2013, Josh was sent back to prison, beginning what will be at least a two-year sentence for crimes that include assaulting a police officer (in November 2012), as well as two counts of Uttering and Publishing and one count of Larceny in a Building, stemming from the felonies he acquired in 2011. His earliest release date is listed as March 8, 2015.

GARY SHIRLEY

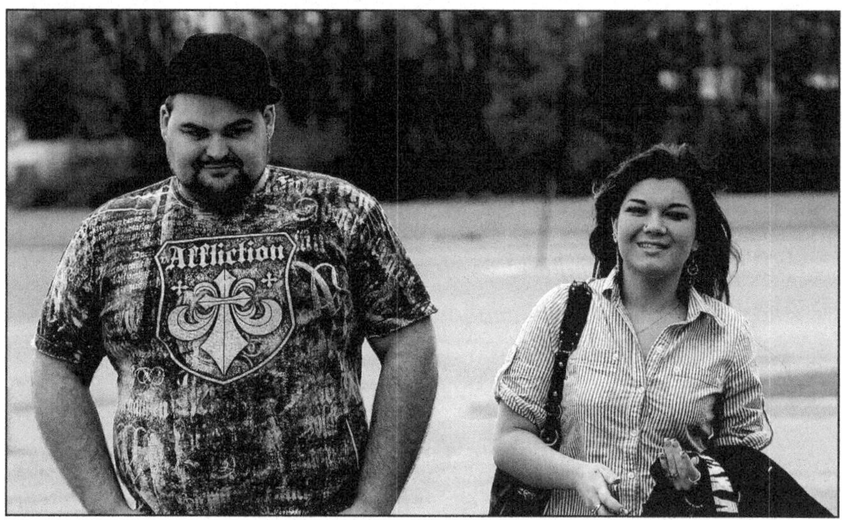

He's been punched by **Amber,** photographed with strippers and blasted online by **Farrah**. **Gary Shirley**, a former lineman for the Anderson High School football team, had no idea his life would become an out-of-control circus of arrests, drugs and custody dramas when he began dating his high school buddy's 15 year-old sister in late 2005. Amber – who was immediately smitten with 19 year-old Gary's teddy bear-like persona – would often sneak into his house for late night romps and a serenade by guitar. But the relationship was tumultuous from the start.

Though Gary – a Certified Nursing Assistant who worked with developmentally disabled patients – declared his love by having Amber's name tattooed on his shoulder in 2011, he often had trouble remaining faithful. Amber, too, enjoyed the company of other men, as the relationship turned more violent and toxic. After Amber suffered a series of legal setbacks, Gary was awarded full custody of their daughter Leah and moved to nearby Noblesville, Indiana in search of a fresh start.

As of March 2013, Gary has not brought Leah to visit her mother in prison, where she is serving up to five years for failing to comply with the terms of a court-ordered drug rehab program, but he says he plans to soon. "It's hard having a kid, especially with an a—hole," Amber revealed in the August 2012 *Teen Mom* series finale. The episode, taped nearly a year earlier, featured an explosive dispute between the exes, during which Gary called Amber a "slut."

After the scene aired, Farrah declared a *Twitter* war on the portly star, publically questioning his ability to parent the three year-old.

> *@FarrahAbraham1: "To be honest Gary is so negative and I don't see how he is better to raise Leah than Amber, get the point Gary! Learn to focus on Leah."*
>
> *@ItsGaryTime: "Seriously Farrah I don't care for you one bit. Your cry face sucks and so do your cookies. Unless you change you are gonna die lonely."*
>
> *@FarrahAbraham1: "What a pig! You're horrible! Go get mental help for Amber's sake P.O.S."*
>
> *@ItsGaryTime: "Go make another hit single or treat your parents like shit. Always stuck up for you but not anymore."*
>
> *@ItsGaryTime: "Sorry Farrah but you need to be nice to people. Sorry for my tweets, not who I am"*

Gary's "Big" Legal Problem

Gary was picked up on May 24, 2011 at 1:34 AM in Alexandria, Indiana for driving on a suspended license – a Class A misdemeanor – and (shocker!) Amber was in the car with him. The official police report states that Gary had pulled over to the side of the road and the pair was overheard arguing.

"I observed a silver Dodge stopped on the south side of Berry Street. I could hear a female arguing with a male inside the vehicle," arresting officer **Kyle Williams** wrote. "I asked the male sitting in the driver seat if everything was ok and he advised yes. The female advised that everything was fine. I advised them that I had heard them arguing and wanted to make sure. I asked them both for identification.... The male introduced himself and the female as Gary Shirley and Amber Portwood from *Teen Mom*.'"

While the crime wasn't that big, Gary – at 5'11" and 300 lbs. – was. "I placed Mr. Shirley in two (2) sets of handcuffs due to his size," the report states. "Both sets of handcuffs were checked for tightness and doubled locked. Capt. Austin stayed with Miss Portwood and the vehicle and arrangements were made for both to be picked up." Gary, who learned his license was suspended in November 2010, was booked at Madison County Jail and released on $3,000 bond.

The Ashley Says...

It's Time For Gary Time – The Show!

Gary is one of the most colorful – and misunderstood – characters in *Teen Mom* history. Over the years, we've seen him take an on-camera punch from Amber, break through the wood stairs of his house, and, thanks to *TMZ*, relish in a 12-hour strip club bender.

I had the unique privilege of spending an evening with Gary in Indianapolis recently and was surprised to see how different he is from the naïve, somewhat oaf-ish guy we saw on TV. Sure lots of people approached him saying "Hey, you're the guy that got beat up on *Teen Mom*." But when you get past that, Gary is just a loving dad, trying to do the best job he can of raising his daughter. He is working towards becoming a Registered Nurse. He also loves to cook and says he would one day like to own a restaurant.

Gary is very aware of how difficult it is for Leah to not have her mother around, and he's very conscious about who he allows to interact with her. I was surprised to see how gracious he is with fans. Seriously, people love him!

During our outing, at least 20 people walked up asking for pictures, and he was happy to pose for each one. He kept me laughing the entire night.

Somebody really needs to give this guy his own single dad spin-off show!

Chapter 13

BUTCH BALTIERRA BEHIND BARS:
THE EXCLUSIVE JAILHOUSE INTERVIEW

Tyler Baltierra was conceived during an emotional night of grief-fueled lust, just hours after his uncle **Dale** died in a horrific drunk driving accident. Tyler's father, **Darl** – who friends and family know simply as "Butch" – had recently separated from his longtime girlfriend, **Kimberly Forbes**, the mother of his then three year-old daughter, **Amber**. But the couple came together again to comfort each other on that tragic night in April 1991, when Dale, 35, broadsided a tree and was killed on impact. "Kim really loved me a lot," the mullet-sporting bad boy says. "She had come over to console me and we got together then. Dale was gone and Tyler got made. Out with the old, in with the new."

Butch – a fence builder, who has spent much of Tyler's life behind bars – admits it was his excessive drug use that eventually prompted Kim to kick him to the curb. Marijuana and cocaine were his drugs of choice. "She just couldn't handle it," the father of two confided during a series of interviews from the Central Michigan Correctional Facility, where he returned in late 2011 after a probation violation. "She just packed my shit one day. I came home and all my stuff was on the front porch. I didn't really care at the time."

Kim, a devout Christian and former Denny's waitress, was Butch's longest lasting love – 12 years – but not his first. He had already lost his virginity by the ninth grade and was chasing skirts all around Chesterfield, Michigan at 16, rarely practicing safe sex. Wearing condoms, he says, "was like taking a shower with a raincoat on. I was just gettin' my freak on. I was tryin' to get the bitches pregnant. I didn't give a fuck about anything... I was a horndog!"

After dropping out of high school, Butch took a job at the Safie pickle factory, a few blocks from his home. It was there the young ladies man struck up a friendship with co-worker **Nick Placencia**, who introduced him to his 16 year-old sister, Tracy. "She was beautiful," Butch recalls. "She was my first love." They dated for nearly four months, but the romance took an unexpected turn when young Butch was introduced to the girl's father, a Ford Motor Company worker with 13 children who was known around town as **Potato Joe**.

"He was pretty much an alcoholic and drug addict," Butch remembers. "And he says to me 'You can't be dating **Tracy** – 'cause she's your sister! You'll have retarded babies.' I was like 'Man, you're high!' So he grabbed a bag of weed, we rolled a joint and went on a dirt road and he was like 'Me and your mother... Look at you. Look at me!' I kind of thought we looked alike, but I was shocked. I'm thinkin' 'This guy is crazy! He's gettin' high on his own supply,' you know? So I went home and asked my father."

It wasn't long before Butch confirmed that much of the life he knew was a lie. His mother, a half-German, half Native American "wild woman" named **Jacqueline Joyce Fritz**, had indeed had an affair with Potato Joe. "She never would admit it, but then my aunt told me it was true," he says. "My whole fucking world was shot. I was mad at the whole world. I hated everybody."

For years, Butch had believed his birth father was a Chevrolet assembly line worker named **Willie Baltierra**, who spent his free time building hot rods with his boys. Willie also had a daughter named **Kimberly** and two other sons, Dale and **William Daryl**. "To me, he was my father," Butch says. "Even though he didn't make me, he made me. He made me the man I am. He gave me a good work ethic. He is hardcore."

Potato Joe, meanwhile, eventually committed suicide. "He bought a 22 and laid in bed and put a pillow over his head and pulled the trigger," Butch says. "He had seven nervous breakdowns." Jacqueline walked out on her family when Butch was just three years old. He was raised by Willie (with occasional help from Willie's live-in girlfriend **Darlene**) in a home environment he likens to being "a dog in a fucking cage."

"There was no 'I love you, son' or 'I love you, brother,'" he says. "I had a lot of issues. I was depressed with my childhood growing up, with my father beating me...all that shit. I remember seeing my mother going through a big picture window when I was three. Layin' on the grass, screamin' and hollerin'. The police coming... There was blood everywhere. The psychologist told me I wasn't supposed to remember that at three years old, but I can tell you all the details – where everyone was standing... I can tell you everything. I can see it right now. In color!"

Butch didn't see his mother again until age 13, when she surprised him near a basketball court in New Haven, Michigan. "She kept yellin'

'Darl, Darl.' And nobody called me Darl. So I walk over and say 'Who are you?' And she says 'I'm your mother.' And she hugged me and kissed me. I was like, 'Damn, I got a mom!' Before that, when I was a kid, I used to lay in my bed and wet the bed every night. My dad beat the shit out of me. He scared me so bad. I didn't know that was why, but that was why. I would sit there thinking 'The only one that loves me is my mother.' I would pray to God, 'I know, Lord, she is the only one that loves me.' I didn't even know the lady. And I would cry myself to sleep and say 'She's the only one that loved me.' Then all of a sudden, bam! She is in my life. Out of the sky."

"I was drinkin' and doin' crack the whole time of the filming. Nobody really knew. Well, I'm sure they knew, but... If you watch the show you knew. But 99% of the time I had beer in me. Or marijuana. That is what I did. I was an alcoholic, drug addict."

- BUTCH BALTIERRA

Butch and his mother remained in contact, mostly by phone, until her death in 1992 from an aneurysm. "She was makin' apple pies and crocheting in a chair, smoking when she died," he says. Like Jacqueline, Butch struggled with substance abuse for much of his adult life. He admits to being stoned or drunk during almost all of his appearances on *16 and Pregnant* and *Teen Mom*. "I was drinkin' and doin' crack the whole time of the filming," he says. "Nobody really knew. Well, I'm sure they knew, but... If you watch the show you knew. But 99% of the time I had beer in me. Or marijuana. That is what I did. I was an alcoholic, drug addict."

Substance abuse has played a role in many of Butch's run-ins with the law. He landed behind bars for the first time at age 24 for snorting cocaine off the glove box of a 1976 canary yellow Cadillac in Capitola, California. His growing rap sheet also includes multiple arrests for breaking and entering as well as charges of domestic violence, larceny, and home invasion. Butch was most recently sent back to jail following a 2011 domestic spat with his current wife, **April**, a chain smoker and former quality control agent. At the time, April claimed that her husband of two years came home under the influence of drugs on the night of September 8, slammed her head into a bathroom wall and tried to choke her with a towel. "He didn't look like himself," April explained during the final season of *Teen Mom*. "I was on the phone with my girlfriend and he thought I was talking to [MY son] Nick's dad and he freaked out on me. I'm all bruised up. I look like I got ran over by a truck."

Butch remembers the episode differently: "She accused *me* of cheatin' on *her*! Normally (in a situation like that) I will just leave. I will say a few things that are derogatory and I try to leave. And she will try to stop me. That is when it gets physical. At that particular one, we were at our neighbor's. Our new neighbors that had just moved into Port Huron. And the girl was pretty hot. We were over there drinkin' a couple of beers and they gave me a quarter of an Oxycontin, which is not my thing. I don't do pills. And she gave me half a Valium. And I am drinkin' Budweiser. When we got home, April accused me of tryin' to get with the neighbor. She grabbed me and I had to stop her from grabbin' and hittin' on me. I got pictures of the scratches on my neck. She stopped me, jumped on my back and all kinds of stuff."

Butch's daughter Amber (b. 1987) wasn't buying his story. She immediately took to the Internet to blast her father for his actions. "I dare someone to try and defend my piece of sh** 'dad' now!!" she wrote on *Facebook*. "Comes home high and beats his fu**ing wife & the best part is the cops caught him red handed!!" A subsequent posting added:

"Drug addicts can't handle TV money. This just goes to show what he cares about. Crack. Bottom line."

Butch Baltierra and his son, Tyler

Butch ended up pleading not guilty and the charges were dropped in January 2012. But he remained a guest of the state since the altercation violated a "no contact" order that was still in place at the time of his arrest. He will be eligible for parole in April 2013. "I don't want people to think I am some kind of woman beater," he insists. "It is very important for me to let people know that. I am not that kind of person. My dad did that stuff, but that is not me. I had that one moment, but beating up defenseless women is not my M.O."

Butch and April's sometimes-turbulent love story began in July 2008. Tyler had been dating Catelynn for several years and she was a frequent guest at the Baltierra house. "I came home on parole and I met Catelynn cause I was stayin' at Tyler's house," Butch remembers. "Catelynn goes 'My mom would like you!' I was like 'Where's she at?' I was man-whoring around anyways. I just got out of jail, looked good. 185 pounds. I was pretty ripped up after doin' Tae Bo for five years." Catelynn put in a good word at home and soon after the two chain smokers were introduced. "She invited me over for Nicholas's second birthday party," he says. "We drank some beers, she jumped in my truck, we hit a few bars, went down a back road and did the country thing."

The couple dated for six months before tying the knot on February 13, 2009 at a small chapel in Warren, Michigan. Tyler was the only member of Butch's family to show up. "I never did ask Amber why she didn't come," he says. "She had something else going on, I guess."

Butch recalls being "pretty fucking drunk" the night before the nuptials. "I didn't get home until about six in the morning," he says. "I left in the middle of the night and went to get high. April thought I had cold feet and left. She was up crying when I got home. Then my daughter (Amber) came over and did her hair. After we got married, we went to Famous Dave's Restaurant. Her father dropped us off at a hotel room and we stayed there all weekend. We were drunk in the hot tub for three days."

But those days are behind him. Butch says he hopes to move into a residential rehab program or sober living facility when he is released. "I don't even smoke cigarettes no more," he says. "I'm pretty proud of that. I've been smoking cigarettes since I was eight years old. I ain't never thought I could [quit]. I'm breaking my arm right now trying to pat myself on the back. There's plenty marijuana in here, plenty of cigarettes, that I could do any time I want. But I'm done. I'm 50 years old and I hit the end of the road. I had a good time, I had a good run. It just wasn't working out very well for me."

BUTCH BALTIERRA: MORE OF THE JAILHOUSE Q&A

Q: What is your current prison experience like?

It is level one, low security. We were just in the news (recently). There are about three to four stabbings a week. It is kind of rough. But I stay busy. I got a P90X class I go to at the gym, three days a week. I hit the gym. I am in pretty good shape for 50 years-old.

Q: Do you have cellmates?

I got about seven. We are in a big cubicle. There ain't much room in there. Four of us on one side and some lockers. Then four more on the other side. I am on the top bunk by the window. I gotta have air. The African Americans like it real hot. People are fartin' and smokin'...

Q: Do the other prisoners know who you are?

Do they know who I am? Yeah, I'm like a big star in here! I'm very well known. Everybody knows who I am.

Q: Have Catelynn or Tyler been to visit you in a while?

No. I talk to him on the phone. He keeps sayin' he is gonna come. But I ain't seen nothing. Last time I was in prison my sister kept sayin' she was coming to visit. She is all I had one time when I was locked up.

Q: What do you think of the way MTV has portrayed you on TV?

They made their own story up. They decided what they wanted it to look and sound like. It wasn't real reality. There is a lot of stuff that wasn't real about it, that was scripted. Which I had a problem with. I am a pretty outspoken person. I am not all that stupid. I do some dumb things, granted. But I think I got a pretty good head on my shoulders as far as being on the streets.

Q: Did they pay you to appear?

Yeah, they pay us by the season. It is really for 10 episodes. So it comes out to about $850 per episode. I told them I wanted $10,000 last time. And they gave me $8,500. They said "We edit you out of most of the episodes."

Q: Does Tyler support you or help you out with money?

No, he don't. I had to beg him -- it took me 6 or 8 weeks -- to get him to give me a [care package]. I finally sent him a form of everything I wanted. Then he fills it all out and put in his credit card information... Then he says "Yeah, Dad, I sent it out and I wrote you a letter." It was the first time he wrote me a letter in the whole year I have been down. He sent me a picture of Carly. I open the letter up and here is the secure pack (order form). It was a good letter. It kind of choked me up. It said, "No matter what, I will always love you." There is a song that we like by Creed, "With Arms Wide Open." When he was 8 years old I told him "This song reminds me of you." The kid does love me. He's just mad at me, I guess. It wasn't like I was gone forever. I was gone for two or three years at a time. But I was always in their life when I was out [of prison]."

Q: What was your first reaction when you met Catelynn? Did you like her?

I am thinkin' "She's alright. He's hittin' it. He's gonna hit that for a while and then get another one. She'll be one of the many that's gonna come in and out." That was my first thought. Tyler was all serious. "I really love her dad. She's the one I want to be with..." I was like "I felt that way when I was 16, too." Then I went and told him the story about his aunt, my sister. [laughs] They have been together ever since. I think maybe they are out to prove something to someone.

Q: Did you ever talk to Tyler about safe sex?

He said he had a rubber in his wallet and he didn't know his mother washed it. He said he'd had it for a long time in there and he used it and evidently it broke.

Q: What was your reaction when he told you Catelynn was pregnant?

We wanted to keep the kid. Catelynn comes to me with her (mother) and April says to me, "Your son got my daughter pregnant." We offered Catelynn... She wanted to abort it. She said, "OK I will." Then I had the money to give her to have it aborted and they started talking to Tyler's mom, and she's a Christian lady. Her name's Kim. She don't believe in abortion. She wanted the kids to give it up for adoption. That went on for a minute and she's telling us the whole time that she's keeping the baby and that we're going to help her and whatever, and I'm into all that. But behind closed doors she went and got a...not a lawyer, but liaison. She went and got one of them to represent her because she was only 16 and she was talking to Bethany Christian adoption agency. In the meantime, we're thinking that she's keeping the kid. I went and got a place, rented a big ol' house on the water. (April's) buying bassinettes. We're all ready to go. Then about a week before she has it she says "I'm going to give the baby up for adoption and here's the people I'm giving it to." You know, she played her mother this whole time. She crushed her mom. And I was pissed. I said, "You don't give your kid away! We don't give our kids away!" She said, "Well I can't take care of it and I don't want it to be around this. I don't want it being around you guys." So I said if you want to give it a better life, give it to her. Him or her, we didn't know what it was. I said, you give it to her. Tyler's telling me this. I told him, "You're the one that can give her a better life. You want to give her to someone else so they can do it? I said I would have stayed in an abandoned car rather than give you motherfucking kids away. We don't do that in our family. He said, "Well I think it's a good idea." I told him that we were there to help them in any way, you know. So it went on like that and I was pretty pissed about it. I didn't talk to the kids for three or four months. We had an attitude about it. He's stubborn, I'm stubborn. Then I had to try to accept it, you know what I mean, so I could get my son back. I said, "OK I'm alright with it. I'm glad you picked who you picked. But I don't know how you can just give your kid away in a parking lot of the fucking hospital. Your first born. I don't understand how you could do it. I said, "This is going to come back and it's going to haunt you for the rest of your life, I want you to know that. He said, "I know I'm doing the best thing for her." I said, "You may be doing a good thing for her but you want this kid to have a silver spoon in its mouth. Be a man and step up to the plate. Cowboy up, as I say, and give it to her. You do it. You want someone else to raise your kid." That's my deal on it. I'm a man. I said, "I'm already a role model on what not to do, Tyler. I'm a living example of what not to be like and what not to do. So you already know what not to do."

Q: In 2012, Catelynn claimed that April sold a false story about her being pregnant to *In Touch* magazine. What really happened?

She told me that her and Catelynn and another girl named Jamie were all going to go in on this and (try to) make some money off of this. Catelynn was okay with it. April thought she could get five grand out of it. Then (*In Touch* magazine) turns around and offers Catelynn and Tyler 12 grand. So that was a scam. It was a hustle. But when they called Catelynn she reneged on her mother. "I couldn't lie, Mom." It cost April five grand. And Jamie was gonna get a couple of grand. So Catelynn kind of stabbed her mother in the back on that one.

UPDATE: MARCH, 2013

Gang Members Try To Kill Butch In Jail

Butch is lucky to be alive after a series of violent jailhouse attacks by members of a southwest Detroit gang. On December 11 2012, he was struck in the head and "knocked out" by a metal lock wrapped inside a tube sock. Several weeks later, Butch tells us, members of the Latin Counts crew snuck up from behind and stabbed him multiple times, leaving cuts on his hands and face. "The next day they told me to get off the yard," he says. "I told them I wasn't goin' nowhere and they'd have to take me out in a body bag. I said 'Let's just fight. I'll take two or three of you in the bathroom.' They didn't want to do that, so they snuck up behind me while I was layin' on my bunk and poured hot sugar water on me. They got me pretty good. Burned the shit out of me. They snuck up behind me. Hit the back of my head and my right back arm. The inside of my scalp got burned pretty good."

After receiving medical treatment, Butch was moved to a different facility, in nearby Jackson, Michigan, for his own safety. The violence began, Butch says, after he confronted gang members who stole a television set from another prisoner who suffers from Cerebral Palsy and is confined to a wheelchair.

Chapter 14

WILL KATIE YEAGER BE THE BREAKOUT STAR OF *TEEN MOM 3*?

Katie Yeager's life story has all the ingredients of a spectacular, runaway train wreck: abusive, cheating boyfriend, incarcerated, drug-dealing father and an unplanned high school pregnancy. But the witty, doe-eyed Wyoming teen who always dreamt of becoming a psychologist – has somehow managed to beat the odds. Now, as she prepares to begin her junior year at the University of Utah in September 2013, and struggles to raise cutie pie daughter **Molli** on her own, the former kiddie pageant queen looks poised to become the breakout star of *Teen Mom 3*.

"Being a part of it has given me an opportunity to be able to show my daughter that her dad and I have struggled and made sacrifices for her simply because we have unconditional love for her," Katie shared in a late 2012 Facebook posting. "I am proud of myself for growing such a thick skin and being brave enough to share my life with such a judgmental and rude world."

The series – premiering later in 2013 – will also peek into the day-to-day dramas of cheerleader **Mackenzie Douthit**, dancer **Alexandria Sekella** and Valencia College freshman **Briana Dejesus**, who all appeared during the fourth season of *16 and Pregnant*. "They picked more wholesome girls this time," a show source reveals. "Each one has a job, family support, and goes to school. None of them have drug addictions or any major psychological damages."

Still, there is plenty of drama to look forward to. Much of Katie's story line will focus on school – she recently received an Associates degree from Western Wyoming Community College – her struggle for independence and the challenges of moving on from hot-tempered baby daddy, **Joey Maes**. The couple called it quits, an insider says, "because Joey had been physically and emotionally abusing her for over a year."

Katie seemed to confirm that report in a blistering March 2013 social media post, apparently referencing the short fused coal mine worker: "When you say it's my fault for staying with him when he was abusive for over a year you're just being inconsiderate. Fear is powerful. Don't pretend like you know the sacrifices I've made and the shame that it has caused me. Rebuilding who you once were isn't easy..." She also re-tweeted messages of support from fans, replying to one by revealing "All the violence is followed with I love you'd and it'll never happen again and then somehow is blamed on you." [sic]

Katie, once a competitive swimmer, told us she is contractually forbidden from giving interviews without permission from MTV. But we were able to track down several people close to the young mom, who say she landed in the hospital in late 2012 with serious bruising and several cracked ribs after a heated altercation with her ex. "That's when she moved out and left him," a childhood friend reveals. "They are civil now." Show sources hint Joey "will be a main focus of the show" as the season progresses.

Several people familiar with Katie and her family say she had a "pretty average" childhood – but things quickly became complicated by the time she started high school. She's the oldest of three children. Sister **Blake** was 16 and brother **Riley** was 14 at press time. Her mother, **Luci**, is a hairdresser; father, **Russell Armstrong**, races cars and runs an auto body shop in Green River, Wyoming. (Both of Katie's parents hate that she is part of *Teen Mom 3* and will rarely be seen on camera.) The family temporarily relocated to a small town near Jackson Hole when Katie was 8, so her father could expand his business.

Katie – a self-described "social butterfly" – spent much of her youth in the pool. She attended swim practice twice each day and competed on two different teams in middle school. "She went to state (championships) each year and was highly ranked," a friend says. The family moved to Green River when Katie was ready to begin high school, hoping she could secure a swimming scholarship. But just two weeks into her freshman year, Katie's life went off the rails when her father was arrested for "Conspiracy To Distribute" Methamphetamine. "[He] wasn't released until I was almost 17," she shared on *Instagram* in early 2013. "We are just now slowly rebuilding our relationship and trust."

Friends say Katie gave up swimming and started hanging out with "all the wrong kind of people" after her father was sent to lockup in El Paso, Texas. "All she wanted to do was party," we're told. "She never experimented with drugs...but went through a phase where she would black out on Friday and wouldn't remember anything until Sunday."

Making matters worse, she was also nursing a broken heart after her first boyfriend, **Coleman**, moved away. "He was the only guy I ever loved," she told friends. Together they shared the heartache of losing their dads and the intimacy of losing their virginity. Coleman headed to Colorado, where he now attends culinary school and owns his own food truck. He has invited Katie to one day join him with the promise they would marry. But deep inside, Katie knows that will probably never happen.

As she lost control of her life, Katie began to sink into a deep depression. During her sophomore year, she started dating an older guy (whose name we have been asked to withhold). Friends say he tried to lead her down a path of drug abuse. On one particular night in December 2008, he invited Katie over to party with him and his best friend. Katie, at the time, was tending to her own best friend after a long night of drinking and declined the offer. A few hours later, her boyfriend's friend was pronounced dead from an overdose of heroin. "That was the night she stopped partying as much and started to focus on herself and school."

Katie had known Joey for most of her life before they started dating. She would often spend summers with her grandparents who lived in the same town as his dad. During their junior year in high school, Joey was sent away to a drug and alcohol treatment center. He returned almost a year later and headed straight to her house. The relationship was casual at first -- mostly hanging out at parties and on the weekends. "It wasn't anything either of them saw going anywhere," a friend remembers.

Katie was more focused on attending college – she was accepted to Denver University, Utah University, Colorado State and Boise State – and Joey planned to enlist in the military after graduation. But things became much more serious when Katie discovered she was pregnant. Almost overnight, she ditched her friends and began spending all of her time with Joey. Panicked and depressed, she concealed the pregnancy from almost everyone until a month before graduation.

Single motherhood is never easy, but Katie seems to be making the best of it. She finished her first year of school with a 3.5 GPA. In October 2012, Katie shared an update on her life via *Twitter*: "Ima mother, work two jobs, going back to college full time, taking online classes to be a certified pharm. tech until I finish school," she wrote. "Taking 2 month pharm tech course so I can make $ while I'm working on my masters." [sic]

She also appears to have finally found love again. In March 2013, Katie posted a shirtless photo of her new man **Scott Eversull**. "He thinks he's so cute sending me pictures of him in MY favorite pants he stole," she wrote. Scott, too, has been sharing online about the red-hot romance, tweeting: "I still remember the first time we kissed." On his official page (discovered by *Wetpaint.com*), Scott reveals: "ive been in trouble for about 3 years now and im not proud if any of it. i recently graduated from red top meadows in wilson. ive learned alot and ive learned to help others." [sic]

According to the school's official website, Red Top Meadows "provides residential treatment and therapeutic wilderness programs for adolescent males with behavioral, emotional and/or mental health issues." Sounds like Katie's new man could add some real spice to her life – but we'll have to wait to see that during season two.

* * * *

WHAT WE LEARNED ABOUT KATIE FROM TWITTER

* She wants to home school her daughter.

After the December 2012 shooting at Sandy Hook Elementary School in Connecticut, Katie told her more than 20,000 followers the tragedy was "one of the many reasons why Molli will be home-schooled. Who shoots kids? Why do we live in a world like this? #PrayForNewtown."

She later followed up, adding: "Makes me sick to my stomach. Whatever happened to schools being a safe place for children to learn."

*** She was the original Honey Boo Boo.**

"#DidYouKnow I did pageants from the time that I was 2 until I was 16," she shared on October 19, 2012. "Yeah I was the original #ToddlersInTiaras." In another post, shared: "I did pageants for so many years that the smell of some hairsprays makes me sick."

*** She has a great sense of humor.**

In February 2013, she wrote: "Baby you're the reason I get up in the morning! Just kidding I need to pee."

*** You don't want to cross her.**

After allegedly catching Joey in the act with a girl named **Brigette**, she gave him a public dressing down: "No, I'm not jealous of your new girlfriend. I feel sorry for her, because she's dating an unfaithful selfish asshole."

MEET THE OTHER GIRLS OF *TEEN MOM 3*

MACKENZIE DOUTHIT

Miami, Oklahoma
(b. October 17, 1994)

Baby: Gannon Dwayne McKee (b. September 12, 2011)
Baby Daddy: Joshua McKee
Episode 401: March 27, 2012

The perky, blonde cheerleader had a hard time keeping her boyfriend, Josh, off the rodeo horse. During her episode, she even considered leaving him due to his refusal to stop riding and get a job to help support their son.

Since we last saw Mackenzie, she's gone back to high school and cheerleading, and she and Josh have had their share of relationship drama. The couple got engaged shortly after their *16 and Pregnant* episode aired, only to call it off the following year and just "go back to dating." In January 2013, Mackenzie announced on her *Facebook* page that Josh had proposed again and that they were planning to marry in April. Josh was planning on joining the military and Mackenzie and Gannon were planning to go with him to California, where he'd be stationed.

Although she had already bought her wedding gown, Mackenzie announced in March 2013 that the wedding was off and she and Josh were over, due to Josh being "too much like his dad," whom Mackenzie does not get along with. However, the couple was back together by the end of the month.

What We'll See On *Teen Mom 3*: Mackenzie and Josh attend their high school prom. We'll watch as Mackenzie tries to juggle motherhood, high school, her relationship and cosmetology school. We will also see Mackenzie attempt to deal with the drama between her and Josh, some of which stands from past infidelities, according to an inside source. In addition, Mackenzie, who was *still* not on birth control during the filming of the first season, is rumored to have a pregnancy scare. Mackenzie also deals with issues relating to her Type I diabetes.

BRIANA DEJESUS

Orlando, Florida
(b. May 24, 1994)

Baby: Nova Star DeJesus (b. September 9, 2011)
Baby Daddy: Devoin Austin II
Episode 403: April 3, 2012

Briana's episode of 16 and Pregnant centered on Briana and her sister, Brittany, both of whom found themselves pregnant as teenagers but ended up making very different choices. Brittany chose to have an abortion, while Briana gave birth to a daughter, Nova, despite the fact that the baby's father wanted nothing to do with Briana or their kid.

After her episode aired, Briana enrolled in community college and got a job at a clothing store. She continues to raise her daughter on her own, with the help of her mother and sister. She has kept a relatively low online profile since her *16 and Pregnant* episode aired. She did, however, share the struggles she faced as a teen mom on her *Twitter* account in March 2013.

"Some people just don't understand that I'm a mother, not a regular teenager... Being a mother has turned me into this freak, like I enjoy doing things just to see a smile... That smile is so rewarding...Being a mother has taught me to be so caring and loving.... I sometimes feel obligated to do too much for others...not good at all!!"

What We'll See On *Teen Mom 3*: Devoin makes an appearance at Nova's first birthday party, despite having been absent for most of his daughter's first year of life. Briana will attempt to venture back into the dating scene, without much success.

ALEXANDRIA SEKELLA

Neffs, Pennsylvania
(b. December 4, 1993)

Baby: Arabella Elizabeth Sekella-McCann (b. July 18, 2011)
Baby Daddy: Matthew McCann
Episode 405: April 17, 2012

When we last saw her, Alex, who blames faulty birth control for her pregnancy, was faced with having nowhere to live, and dealing with a boyfriend that was more into getting high than taking care of their daughter. (Who could forget the scene in her *16 and Pregnant* episode in which she goes to his house, in labor, and begs him to come to the hospital with her?)

Since her episode aired, life has gotten better for Alexandria, who has moved back in with her mother, and is teaching at a dance school. Her baby's father, Matt, is no longer involved in Arabella's life. (In February 2013, she posted on her *Facebook* page that it had been over a year since Matt had seen his daughter.)

In December 2012, Matt was with friends at a local Pennsylvania party spot known as "The Knob," when he walked off a cliff and broke his neck and back. After a stay in the intensive care unit, he made a full recovery.

What We'll See On *Teen Mom 3*: Alex struggles to raise her daughter alone, while dealing with Matt's antics. Although they are no longer together, Matt continues to make life hard for Alex. His rumored continued drug use will make Alex pursue — and get — full custody of their daughter. Alex tries to balance work, school and single motherhood.

The Ashley Says...

Katie, *Teen Mom 3* Girls Can Turn the Franchise Around

Producers were wise to pick girls, like Katie, that are on "the right track" for *Teen Mom 3*. Their past decisions to choose the most volatile and provocative girls (Hello, Jenelle!) pretty much backfired if you ask me. Although a good smack down or custody battle is great for ratings, they also create heaps of legal problems and bad publicity.

Katie seems like a girl that could have gone off the rails, given everything she has been through. But she managed to keep her head on straight and make a better life for herself and her daughter. I don't believe the girls on these shows should be looked up to as role models, but we can't pretend that young girls don't watch these shows and look up to their stars. I'm happy to see that MTV finally realized this and appears to be attempting to bring the brand back to its original purpose—showing the trials and tribulations of young motherhood.

Chapter 15

WHERE ARE THEY NOW?
MORE AMAZING STORIES OF LIFE AFTER THE CAMERAS LEFT

EBONY JACKSON HAS A MENTAL BREAKDOWN, THEN A BABY!

Ebony Jackson-Rendon didn't have much to say after her shocking September 2011 arrest for endangering the welfare of a minor, possession of drug paraphernalia, maintaining a drug premise, and unauthorized use of another's property to facilitate a crime. Her daughter **Jocelyn**, just two, had been hauled off by Child Protective Services after the young mom and husband **Joshua** were discovered living in a house reportedly covered in flies and feces. "Many people wanted to do an interview with us," she remembers. "But we didn't want to." Until now.

For the first time ever, Ebony is opening up about the dark times and personal demons she faced in the years after her appearance on *16 and Pregnant*. "I was diagnosed with manic depression," she reveals. "I am fine now. They have me on medication. I was on depression medication for a while and it just made everything completely worse. It was just a downhill spiral for me."

Baby Josiah James is laid to rest.

Things began to unravel in May 2011, when Ebony developed an ectopic pregnancy and suffered a painful miscarriage. "We were trying to have another kid at that time, so losing the baby was really hard on me," she admits. A month later, Ebony and Josh – a member of the United States Air Force – held a small, private funeral for their unborn child, "but it wasn't the closure I thought it would be," she says. Ebony continued to grieve privately for months, becoming more and more despondent and neglecting simple tasks like cleaning the home they shared on a Little Rock, Arkansas military base. "What my doctor explained to me is that when I would have a manic episode, everything in my day-to-day life would just not seem the way that it was," she explains. "I just stopped doing the dishes every day."

Eventually state health investigators came knocking. Per their official report:

During the search, Detectives located approximately 1 gram of synthetic marijuana along with several empty packages of synthetic marijuana. Paraphernalia in the form of a variety of smoking devices (pipes) and deplorable conditions in the house. Every room inside the residence had human and dog feces on the floors, walls and clothing. The house was full of flies, and in some areas, maggots. Animal control was called to retrieve 3 dogs that had been inside the house."

"There was just a lot that was on our plate at the time," Ebony admits. "But nothing that was said about our daughter not being taken care of... that was in no way true." Ebony insists that media reports were strongly exaggerated and says her daughter even got a clean bill of health from her doctor the very morning authorities arrived at the home. She also offers some new and more detailed insight into the what the family's living conditions were really like. "The fact that they said there was dog feces everywhere on the carpet was not true," Ebony tells us. "There was stains from the puppies. They said there was human feces on the wall. In part that was true. But it was because my daughter was a toddler and she had taken off her diaper. I don't know what her fascination was with pooping... Of course we did clean it up. What they did was they pulled her dresser away from the wall. And we put it there for a reason. Because she had dug [her poop] into the wall with a stick or something. Like a popsicle stick. And it was just... We didn't have the paint to cover it up and we tried to wash it away, but it was taking off the paint on the wall... And they just made it seem way worse than it actually was."

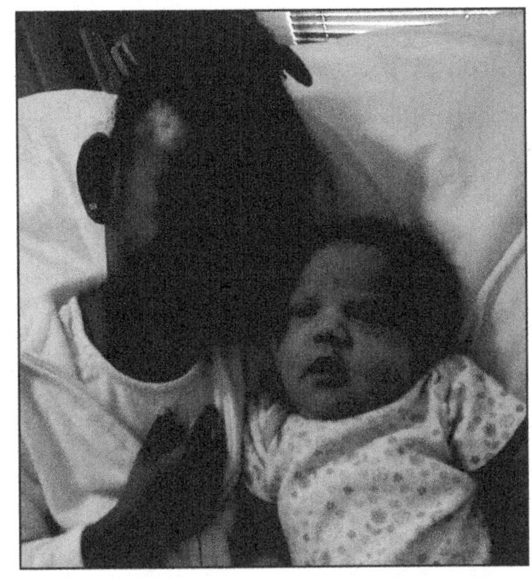

Ebony's daughter Jocelyn and new baby sister Jayda Jewell

Ebony says her story was leaked to the media by someone who was pretending to be her friend. "She wanted to get everything she could out of the story," Ebony says. "They ended up finding the synthetic marijuana in the house – it was actually hers! She brought it over to our house because her husband came home from Korea and she decided that 'I am just gonna leave this over here.' The paraphernalia that was in the house was hers too. It ended up all on our plate. We couldn't really say it was hers, though [because] nobody would have believed it."

Despite Ebony's objections and explanations, Jocelyn was sent to live with a foster family 30 minutes away for the next six months. "Everybody thought the worst of us – that we were just awful parents," she remembers. "But in fact, we were such good parents to Jocelyn, we had her back in six months. Even Jocelyn's lawyer said she was so proud of us for how we had grown up and taken responsibility for our actions."

But the road to recovery wasn't easy. Just weeks after Jocelyn was taken away, Ebony hit rock bottom. "I was in a hospital for having a mental breakdown," she admits. "It wasn't for drugs. My father said that to a newspaper for some reason. I have no idea what his problem was. But it was a real hospital. I just needed to feel better and what they were giving me just wasn't right, so... I got the counseling I needed and I am still seeing a counselor to this day."

Now, one piece at a time, Ebony's life is slowly coming together. In October 2012, she welcomed another baby, **Jayda Jewell**. "It was kind of an accident that we got pregnant again," she confesses. "I was very scared at the beginning. We had a scare because my stomach started hurting like it did when I had the miscarriage. It just felt like it was going to happen all over again. I started crying, but then they did an ultrasound. And they said the baby was exactly where she was supposed to be and she was a very healthy little girl when she was born. Very healthy. I think she overcooked! She came out eight pounds, two ounces." The couple were hoping for a boy, she admits, but Jocelyn has quickly grown fond of her new baby sister. "The next time -- which will be in like five years -- it will be a boy," she says.

Ebony, Josh and the two girls left the base in 2012 and currently reside with Josh's family in New Mexico. Jocelyn began pre-school in January 2013. Josh has left the Air Force and now travels from state to state working as an auto detailer. And, in a twist of irony, Ebony recently completed a program to become a certified dog trainer.

"Whenever things get really hard, me and Josh get closer together," she beams. "A lot of couples would fall apart in the situations we have been through. We have been through quite a lot in our five years. We don't just give up. It is easier to leave than to stay together. We are a really good couple. With our friends, we are the "old couple" in the group. We are three years married now. I think we are just really compatible with each other. We have our kids to keep us sane. Two kids can make you fall apart too, but even if we fight, we don't go to bed mad."

JAMIE McKAY CHOOSES ABORTION

Jamie McKay had just about gotten her life back together. The pretty North Carolina teen – who shared the journey of her pregnancy with daughter **Miah** during season three – had graduated high school, bought a car and finally moved into a place of her own. Then, just days before beginning her first semester of college, Jamie found herself pregnant. Again.

Jamie McKay and daughter, Miah

Just 18, she knew it would be next to impossible to support two children while juggling classwork and working a minimum wage job as a sandwich artist at Subway. It was lack of money, after all, that she blames – in part – for the unwanted pregnancy. "I kept forgetting my Depo shot and couldn't afford to pay $30 for it," she says. "So I was going to get the Implanon [contraceptive implant]. I got pregnant right after I missed my Depo appointment."

So, like many other girls in her position, Jamie decided to end the pregnancy. It's what happened next that sent shockwaves through the *Teen Mom* universe. Just days before the presidential election, Jamie posted a sonogram of her aborted fetus on *Twitter* with a message that read: "Rest in peace little angel. September 17, 2012."

"A lot of people think I shouldn't have made that public but I felt like I was keeping a secret," she says. "And I didn't have anyone to talk to. I felt so alone in my situation and I was so depressed. But afterwards people came to me with their stories and all this love and support. I felt so much better. I don't care about the hate because I don't feel so alone anymore and I can relate to others."

Jamie insists she posted the photograph "to honor" the child. "I didn't want to hide it anymore," she tells us. "But a lot of people were disgusted and thought it was sick. Even though I don't, I didn't want to offend anyone. So I took it down. Abortion is a touchy subject."

Jamie says she and her longtime boyfriend **Ryan McElrath**, 20, were "seriously thinking" about adoption, but ultimately opted against it. "Ryan goes out of town for months at a time. He was gone and I would find myself passed out while Miah was playing. She saw me sick and knew something was wrong. I had to drop two classes because I was always sick. Then my dad heard [I was pregnant] through the grapevine and wouldn't answer my phone calls. I knew my mom would tell me to abort it. She wanted me to abort Miah. I felt it was best for my daughter and school to terminate the pregnancy and focus on getting into a better place."

Ryan – who Jamie calls "an amazing father" – drove his longtime girlfriend to a clinic not far from her home, where the couple had to navigate past a small gathering of protestors.

Inside the waiting room, "some girls were crying," she remembers. "Some were just sitting there. I talked to a few of them. They all had reasons for why they couldn't handle another child. Some were on their second abortion." During the procedure, Jamie says she broke down in tears. "I cried. I screamed 'No!' – but I knew it was too late because I had already taken the medicine," she remembers. "Afterwards I left as fast as I could and cried a lot."

In a series of social media postings months later, Jamie – who now uses the Implanon contraceptive implant -- admitted that she sometimes regrets the decision to end her pregnancy. "I feel like I made a mistake and I can't take it back," she wrote. "I have had this in my heart and it has been very hard on me. I was afraid to be judged by my family, my mother, even my dad. So I did it before they could find out. I should have looked into my options more but I didn't."

Now, Jamie says, all she can do is try to move forward. "I want to graduate college," she says. "I am going to be a radiation therapist. It has taken me longer that I have thought, but I am not giving up. I want to own my own home. I want to be in a career where I can come home and help Miah with homework and make dinner and just be there for her. I always said I want to be a soccer mom."

NICOLE FOKOS: SAVED FROM LIFE OF ADDICTION

Nicole Fokos

Nicole found her knight in shining armor just in the nick of time. The high school dropout featured during season two broke up with her boyfriend, **Tyler Keller**, not long after the birth of their daughter, **Brooklyn**, in January 2010. "I fell out of love with him," she says. "I wasn't happy anymore. Things went downhill from there." As the Florida teen tells it, her life quickly spun out of control. She began "partying every night" and abusing drugs and alcohol. "I made a lot of bad choices," she admits. "I was always drunk or high...When you are on drugs, you don't care about anything and your mind is all messed up."

Nicole says getting access to booze, pot and other substances was never a problem at gatherings in her Orlando-area neighborhood. "I never really paid for anything," she says. "I would just go to parties where they had drugs. I am a girl, you know? But I never, ever slept with somebody for drugs. [When] you are a girl, you kind of have the upper hand. Go to a party where there are drugs and they will give it to you."

In 2011, Nicole made the heartbreaking decision to place then one year-old Brooklyn in the day-to-day care of Tyler's grandmother, Nell. "There is no point in making Brooklyn suffer because I can't take care of her the way grandma does," she says. The voluntary arrangement allowed her daughter to receive proper care while Nicole searched for a permanent place to live and a way to support herself.

That's when mutual friends introduced Nicole, 18, to **Kenny**, a 25 year-old contractor who would quickly turn her life around. "He doesn't even smoke cigarettes," she reveals. "He told me, 'If you want to be my friend and hang out with me, you can't do that kind of stuff.' Now he is my boyfriend. I live with him and I have been clean for a year because of him."

Kenny is Nicole's first "real relationship" since Tyler, who she is no longer in contact with. "I had a few boyfriends that would last a few months. But this is the first one that is serious -- where I would say 'I love you' and live with him and share money." Kenny, she says, also helped convince her to walk away from a lucrative job serving cocktails at popular Orlando strip club.

Within a week of her employment at the Diamond Club, the shy teen mom was being recruited by her bosses to go topless for customers and provide exotic private dances. "I was like, 'No!' Every time they asked me," she remembers. "They do that to all the girls though." Most strip club dancers, she says, "are drug addicts and need to make their money to buy their drugs. Some of them have like three kids and they are young and they just need money to feed their kids."

While quitting the job was a financial setback for Nicole, she decided to use the opportunity to work toward completing her G.E.D. In February 2013, Nicole obtained her high school G.E.D., as well as her C.P.R. and first aid certification. As of press time, she is currently working towards her Certified Nursing Assistant license. "It has been my dream for a while to be a nurse," she says. "So I am going to go through with it. I plan to go to nursing school."

Nicole also expects to regain custody of her daughter soon. "But in order for me to get her back, I wanna be back on my feet so I can be better able to take care of her," she says. "Kenny really wants me to get her back. He just wants me to do the right thing. That is what makes me so happy about him."

47 girls have been featured on *16 and Pregnant*. We've followed eight of them as they continued their journeys on *Teen Mom* and *Teen Mom 2*. (*Teen Mom 3* – featuring **Mackenzie**, **Alexandria**, **Briana** and **Katie** – will premiere in 2013.) So what happened to everyone else?

Some have gotten arrested. Others have gotten married. And a few have tried to distance themselves from the shows altogether.

Here's what we've been able to dig up:

- SEASON ONE -

WHITNEY PURVIS

Rome, GA
(b. December 4, 1991)

Baby: Weston Owen Gosa Jr. (b. April 2, 2009)
Baby Daddy: Weston Gosa
Episode 105: July 9, 2009

At 18 months, Weston, Jr. was still receiving CAT scans and was unable to speak properly. Whitney completed her GED, got a job at a local pizza shop and enrolled in college, hoping to become a registered nurse. **Meemaw** (her grandmother) discovered she had breast cancer and began receiving chemotherapy. And though they once planned on getting married, Whitney and Weston -- who both suffered humiliating arrests in 2012 (see chapter 7) – decided to call it quits. "[He] was gone all the time," Whitney told *TMZ*. "He wouldn't come home until 3 AM. I was home with the baby and he was nowhere to be found... He was just out with his friends all the time getting messed up. I don't want that around my kid." They recently got back together and are now living together with their son. Whitney is currently working at a HoneyBaked ham store, while Weston is attending college.

- SEASON TWO -

NIKKOLE PAULUN

Monroe, MI
(b. September 29, 1993)

Baby: Lyle Thomas Drummonds (b. November 5, 2009)
Baby Daddy: Josh Drummonds
Episode 202: February 23, 2010

Nikkole enrolled at the University of Toledo to study nursing while Josh rode it out for five months in jail on larceny charges. After his release, they reconciled (again) and Nikkole and Lyle briefly moved in with Josh. In 2011, Josh was sentenced to 12 more months in the slammer for forging checks from his *own mother's* bank account. When he got out in April 2012, the couple reconciled and moved in together with their son. Things were going so well that by October, Nikkole and Josh got engaged. The engagement was short-lived, however. Nikkole admitted to cheating on Josh later that month, and they split once again. In February 2013, Jenelle Evans announced that Nikkole was pregnant with her second child. Nikkole later backed up Jenelle's claim by posting photos of her baby bump on her *Twitter* and *Instagram* accounts. According to Jenelle, the father of Nikkole's baby is allegedly the guy that she cheated on Josh with back in November 2012.

VALERIE FAIRMAN

Oxford, PA

Baby: Nevaeh Lynn Fairman (b. September 14, 2009)
Baby Daddy: Matt (Last name unknown)
Episode 203: March 2, 2010

Valerie and her baby-daddy split in early 2011 after an on-and-off again relationship. In April of that year, 17-year-old Valerie was arrested and held at a Pennsylvania youth detention center for several days after she assaulted her adoptive mother, **Janice**. She was briefly sent to live at a residential home. As of late 2012, her baby's father was believed to be at a Pennsylvania rehab facility, battling addiction.

LORI WICKELHAUS

Fort Thomas, KY
(b. January 15, 1992)

Baby: Aidan Benson (b. December 16, 2009)
Baby Daddy: Cory Haskett
Episode 204: March 9, 2010

Lori is studying nursing at Eastern West Virginia Tech and working as a Certified Nursing Assistant at a nursing home in West Virginia. Her son, Aidan, who she placed for adoption, lives near her parents' home in Kentucky. She and her family are able to maintain a close relationship with him. She's single and is no longer in contact with her baby's father. Cory is working at an auto parts store and expecting a baby with his new girlfriend in 2013.

SAMANTHA HERNANDEZ

Rosenberg, TX
(b. August 22, 1992)

Baby: Jordynn Amelia Marie Salinas (b. December 22, 2009)
Baby Daddy: Eric Salinas
Episode 206: March 23, 2010

As of November 2012, Samantha and Eric were still living together with their daughter. Samantha graduated high school and has been working at a telecommunications company. She also finally got her driver's license – at age 20. Baby Jordynn continues to receive treatment for joint problems (discovered in early 2011) and has undergone multiple surgeries.

LIZZIE WALLER-SICKLES

Smitherfield, VA
(b. March 9, 1992)

Baby: Summer Jayde Sickles (b. January 30, 2010)
Baby Daddy: Skylar Sickles
Episode 209: April 13, 2010

After marrying Skylar in a small beach ceremony in June 2010, Lizzie went to school to become a dental assistant – but she ended up working at a sky diving facility in Virginia. Lizzie now holds a Type A skydiving license, which means she no longer has to jump with an instructor. Skylar and Lizzie have separated and are no longer living together, although both remain in their daughter's life. Lizzie is currently dating someone new.

BROOKE SMITHERMAN-TARRANT

Mansfield, TX
(b. March 26, 1992)

Baby: Brody Ryan Tarrant (b. January 28, 2010)
Baby Daddy: Cody Tarrant
Episode 211: October 26, 2010

Brooke and Cody have been married for more than three years and continue to live in the Mansfield, Texas barn house featured on *16 and Pregnant*. In December 2012, Brooke gave birth to her second child, daughter **Ryley Jean**. Brooke is employed at a daycare center and Cody works at a machine shop.

FELICIA COOKE

Lewisville, TX
(b. December 16, 1992)

Baby: Genesis Alexa Gutierrez (b. February 25, 2010)
Baby Daddy: Mauricio "Alex" Gutierrez
Episode 212: November 2, 2010

After becoming the first (and only) person from her family to graduate from high school, Felicia broke up with Alex. As of December 2012, she was in a new relationship. Alex had another child with the girl he began seeing after Felicia. They both still live in Texas.

EMILY MCKENZIE

Hayden, AL
(b. August 3, 1993)

Baby: Liam Allen Peterson (b. February 17, 2010)
Baby Daddy: Daniel Peterson
Episode 213: November 9, 2010

Emily and Daniel married shortly after filming their episode – but the relationship never stood a chance. "After having Liam, we just got to that comfortable stage, and being in love didn't seem to matter anymore," she told *RadarOnline* in November 2010. "We got out of the honeymoon stage before even getting married. And it sucks." During the "Where Are They Now?" special, Emily said that she and Daniel were pressured into marriage by their families, and that she was unhappy from the start. Soon after, Emily and Liam moved to Emily's mother's house and the couple separated. In October 2011, her father, Stacey, died suddenly from a heart attack, leaving Emily and her family stunned. In July 2012, Emily and Daniel made their divorce official.

MARKAI DURHAM

Riverview, FL
(b. December 2, 1991)

Baby: Za'Karia Sanari Worsham (b. October 12, 2009)
Baby Daddy: James Worsham
Episode 214: November 16, 2010

Markai was publically ridiculed when she chose to end her second pregnancy on the controversial "No Easy Decision" abortion special in 2010. Soon after, she and James ended their relationship, but they remain friends for the sake of their daughter. Markai now lives in Tampa and works at a cable company. She's currently in school and hopes to become a dental hygienist. According to posts on her *Twitter* account, she plans to get butt implants in 2013. In February 2012, Markai was arrested in Florida for driving on a suspended license and later released on a $250 bond. James, who is still sporting his trademark dreadlocks, graduated from trade school in 2010 and is very much involved in his daughter's life.

AUBREY WOLTERS

Prescott Valley, AZ
(b. July 1, 1992)

Baby: Austin Carter Akerill (b. February 6, 2010)
Baby Daddy: Brandon Akerill
Episode 215: November 23, 2010

Aubrey and Brandon moved to Washington to live with Brandon's father but divorced in February 2011, just before their first anniversary. Video footage from a "Where Are They Now?" special in 2011, showed an underage Aubrey drinking in a nightclub, dancing on a pool table, and talking about becoming a stripper. She told MTV that she was "taking a semester off" from school, but in reality, she had dropped out of college. A few days after the special aired, she took to her *Facebook* fan page to defend her actions: "I'm with my son all week minus a few hours on Thursdays and that's all I focus on," she wrote. "I party on the weekends. Also I've never been drunk when my child is present or even home. I'm not putting him in jeopardy. I don't drink that regularly anyhow." In July 2011, Aubrey revealed that she had a massive tumor in her throat that left her in constant pain and unable to eat or sleep. She lost a great deal of weight, causing fans of the show to speculate that she was abusing drugs. The tumor turned out to be non-cancerous but Aubrey didn't have it removed until late 2011 because she didn't have health insurance. Aubrey now resides in Washington with her son and is on good terms with

Brandon, who lives nearby and works as a bouncer at a bar.

CHRISTINNA COOK

Huntsville, AL

Baby: Destiny Brianna Robinson (b. December 22, 2009)
Baby Daddy: Isaiah Robinson
Episode 216: November 30, 2010

Christinna claims she married – then quickly divorced – Isaiah after he beat her up! The violent scene allegedly played out just a few months before her episode aired. "We got into an argument and it got physical," she revealed on Formspring. "I called the police. They arrested him and the policeman pressed charges then I went to the hospital and had to get surgery and we got back together after that, [which I know was] stupid!" Isaiah, a former high school football star, was charged with third degree assault. After the divorce, Christinna moved to Buffalo, New York to be near her family. Isaiah briefly joined her, but ended up moving back to Alabama. In December 2010, she shared her future plans with *RadarOnline*: "I want to obtain my Masters Degree and establish a career for myself. I want to buy a house in a good neighborhood and school district and find a good church to raise Destiny in. I also want to have more children because I love being a mother. I want to find a good husband, who also has a career and shares the same values that I do and someone to be a father to Destiny since Isaiah has unfortunately chosen not to be a part of Destiny's life. Even if I do not remarry, I just want to be successful so I can give Destiny the best life I possibly can."

KAYLA JORDAN

Centre, AL
(b. December 29, 1992)

Baby: Rylan Jayce Davis (b. January 19, 2010)
Baby Daddy: J.R. Davis
Episode 217: December 7, 2010

Kayla called off her engagement to J.R. shortly after her episode was filmed. Soon after, her parents split up. "I would probably still be that spoiled child that was fed with the preverbal silver spoon if it wasn't for [my parents'] divorce," she wrote on a personal blog in October 2011. "I appreciate the adult that I had to grow into." In November 2011, she began dating someone new. (They were still together a year later!) J.R. is still involved in Rylan's life and now works with his father at the family's carpet business. As of December 2012, Kayla was working part-time at a restaurant and attending college.

MEGAN MCCONNELL

Ault, CO
(b. May 21, 1993)

Baby: Blake Ray Stone (b. January 19, 2010)
Baby Daddy: Nathan Stone
Episode 218: December 14, 2010

Megan married Nathan in February 2011, but the honeymoon didn't last long. By summer, the military brat had discovered that her man – after ditching his promise to enlist – had been texting about her with other girls. "I was completely oblivious to the fact that things were bad," she told *The Ashley's Reality Roundup* in an August 2011 interview. "I guess he's just a good liar." On her personal blog, Megan also hinted that she had suffered some physical abuse:

> *"He has left a few bruises on me. The most recent time was when I confronted him about the texting. He didn't hit me, he just grabbed my arms and left bruises on the back of my arms where he was holding on. The only other time was back in June, he back handed me on my chest and left a bruise. Both times he said these exact words "I'm so sorry baby I will never do it again". That's what pushed me over the edge and lead me to make this decision. No one should have to go through that. It's a terrible feeling. That is why I got my new tattoo on my chest, because every time I see it, it will remind me to learn from my mistakes and never allow myself to get into a bad relationship again.*

Megan filed for divorce after just seven months and says Nathan tried to convince her father to adopt Blake. As of October 2012, Megan was living with her parents in Colorado and attending college full time. She hopes to attend nursing school. As of March 2013, Megan was dating a guy named Lando. Nathan married the girl with whom he was cheating on Megan.

ASHLEY SALAZAR

McKinney, TX
(b. December 1, 1991)

Baby: Callie Danielle Salazar (b. December 16, 2009)
Baby Daddy: Justin Lane
Episode 219: December 21, 2010

In 2011, Ashley got her own apartment, enrolled at The University of North Texas and appeared on a *16 and Pregnant* adoption special to discuss the decision to give up her daughter. "I hope to be at peace [with my choice] as much as Catelynn is someday," she told *The Ashley's Reality Roundup*. "But I am better off with the adoption. I just realized that not much can be changed so I have to make the best with what I have." In January 2012, Ashley released her memoir, *Bittersweet Blessing*, shortly before reuniting with ex-boyfriend Justin, who had never seen their daughter. As of March 2013, Ashley was living in Texas and is in her last year of college. She is still with Justin, who had to relocate to Louisiana to take a job with an oil company. Ashley plans to join him. Being on the show "is harder than it seems," she revealed in a 2011 interview. "You are in such an emotional time of your life and the cameras sometimes got overwhelming. I would also worry what Callie would think about the episodes in the future. I would just tell myself it was for a good cause. That was the hardest part; that and knowing millions would be watching and judging."

- SEASON THREE -

JORDAN WARD-FINDER

St. Louis, MO
(b. February 14, 1993)

Baby: Noah James Finder (b. July 14, 2010)
Baby Daddy: Brian Finder
Episode 301: April 19, 2011

Jordan married Brian in January 2011 and quickly discovered she was pregnant again. A few months after taping the reunion special (in which Jordan did not discuss her second pregnancy), Brian joined the Air Force and the family moved to a base in Monterrey Bay, California. In November 2011, Jordan gave birth to a daughter named **Arri Monroe Finder**. Although Jordan's twin sister, **Jessica**, wasn't able to be in the room for the birth as she was for Noah's, she did watch it via Skype. In September 2012, the family moved to an Air Force base in San Antonio, Texas. A stay-at-home mom, Jordan has said she would like to finish school before having more kids.

JENNIFER DEL RIO

Riverview, FL
(b. October 20, 1993)

Babies: Joshua Devan and Noah Matthew Smith (b. October 11, 2010)
Baby Daddy: Joshua Smith
Episode 302: April 26, 2011

For a while, Jennifer and the twins were living in Chicago, where she spoke to high school students about pregnancy through an organization called Teen Choices International. In July 2012, Jennifer filed legal documents to gain sole custody of the boys, claiming that Josh was a threat to her safety. "I love my two sons with all of my heart, my love for them is out of this world," Josh says. "Sometimes we will learn that we have to slow down in order to move further. My plans, dreams and goals for my children are huge. I know they are in safe hands right now and I will continue let God be in control." Jennifer has since moved back to Riverview and is currently attending college. She is majoring in criminal justice and plans to go into law enforcement. As of March 2013, Josh was back in the twins' lives, with Jennifer even allowing him to have the boys over the weekend. They are now civil to each other and get along for the sake of their children.

DANIELLE CUNNINGHAM

Pataskala, OH
(b. January 7, 1994)

Baby: Jamie Paul Alderman, Jr. (b. October, 2010)
Baby Daddy: Jamie Paul Alderman
Episode 305: May 10, 2011

Jessica Danielle Cunningham immediately considered having an abortion when she became pregnant with her second child in October

2012 – at age 19. "But a week went by and I just couldn't even imagine (doing it)," she wrote on her official *Facebook* fan page. "There's no way I could do it." Danielle – who holds jobs at Target and Tim Horton's – discovered she was about to become a mother again shortly after rekindling her turbulent love affair with Jamie. "[It took] a while to process," her mother Casey tells us. "I guess I can't change anything so I will be happy." Danielle lobbied hard to be included in the *Teen Mom 3* spinoff, which will air in 2013. When she wasn't selected, Danielle began to focus on obtaining her GED and plans to start college in the spring of 2013 – right around her due date! "This baby was placed in my life for a reason and I'm more than willing to start fresh and know it's time to grow up," Danielle posted. "Yes I should [have grown up] before [getting pregnant] but I was also 15 the last time I got pregnant. I'm now 19, and I'm more than excited for my family to grow." Casey, however, remains concerned. "Her life story was just too close to my own and I don't want her to continue this cycle," she says. "I am hoping Jamie stands tall and does what he needs to, so that we can change the page to this story and continue on in a different direction." In February 2013, Danielle announced that she was having a girl, whom she plans to name Jayleigh Danielle. She is expected to give birth in the summer of 2013. She is no longer in a relationship with Jamie.

CLEONDRA CARTER

Horn Lake, MS
(b. June 21, 1993)

Baby: Kylee Sue Escovedo (b. November 29, 2010)
Baby Daddy: Mario Escovedo
Episode 305: May 17, 2011

Cleondra tells us she's "never been happier." After a domestic dispute turned physical and cops were called in late 2011, Cleondra and

Mario went the extra mile to rebuild their relationship. "(We) have our differences but there is no need to throw our family in the trash because of it. We are very stubborn but we've worked on that. Now we do not even go to sleep or leave the house mad at each other. If we are fighting, we work it out." The couple – both work full time while Cleondra studies photography in college – say they plan to marry, but have not yet set a date. "The best part about my filming was just getting my word out there, and showing teen moms that you can do it!" she says. "It is very possible. I have never once looked at my situation and thought, 'Well I'm screwed.' I make the best of it. That's why I am so happy all of the time."

KAYLA JACKSON

Winthrop, MN
(b. March 8, 1993)

Baby: Preston Michael Schwing (b. November 4, 2010)
Baby Daddy: Michael Schwing
Episode 306: May 24, 2011

Shortly after her episode aired, Kayla and Mike split and she moved into an apartment with her friend and baby Preston. Mike eventually moved in, and he and Kayla got back together. They became engaged in March 2012, but by the end of the year had split again. Kayla currently works full-time and shares custody of Preston with Mike. At press time, Kayla was not enrolled in college, although she plans to go at some point in the near future.

IZABELLA TOVAR

Draper, UT
(b. March 15, 1995)

Baby: Enrique Jairo Rodriguez (b. September 17, 2010)
Baby Daddy: Jairo Rodriguez
Episode 307: May 31, 2011

Izabella is currently a senior at a private Catholic high school in Utah. She's an excellent student and currently a member of the National Honor Society. She plans to graduate in 2013, go to the University of Utah and then medical school to become a psychologist. After the episode aired, Jairo got his GED and began a full-time job, which alleviated the tension between him and Izabella's father. In March 2013, Izabella and Jairo announced that they will be getting married on June 8, 2013. In October 2012, Izabella announced that she had changed Enrique's name to Henry (the English version of "Enrique") because it's easier for everyone to pronounce.

KIANNA RANDALL

Fort Worth, TX
(b. June 12, 1993)

Baby: Kay'den Elijah Hegab (b. October 18, 2010)
Baby Daddy: Zak Hegab
Episode 308: June 7, 2011

A few months after her episode aired, Kianna announced on *Twitter* that she was pregnant again. (She later claimed to have miscarried.) In August 2011, Kianna and Zak along with her baby's father, Zak, and several friends, went on a two-day crime spree. On August 20, 2011, she was charged with Burglary of Habitation after attempting to steal items from a man's house in Euless, Texas. That same day, according to police records, Kianna and her crew committed two more armed robberies, using a gun to threaten the victims. The next day, Kianna and her friends went back to Euless and attempted to break into a woman's home. Kianna was charged with four felonies: two counts of Aggravated Robbery, one count of Attempted Burglary or Habitation and one count of Burglary of Habituation, and received 10 years' probation for her crimes. In 2012, her probation was revoked. Zak is currently in a juvenile detention facility in Texas. He was sentenced to 15 years behind bars for his role in the crimes.

TAYLOR LUMAS

Cincinnati, OH
(b. August 16, 1995)

Baby: Aubri Rose Bridewell (b. November 11, 2010)
Baby Daddy: Nathan Bridewell
Episode 309: June 14, 2011

Taylor, the youngest girl ever to be featured on *16 and Pregnant,* is still in high school and recently got her first job and her driver's license. Taylor and Nathan have been on-and-off since her episode aired. As of March 2013, they are together, after having been broken up for nearly a year. Their daughter has suffered from various ailments since she was born and in 2011, had to have surgery to remove a mass from her lung. She made a full recovery.

ALLIE MENDOZA

Pasadena, TX
(b. October 18, 1994)

Baby: Aydenn Anthony Aranzeta (b. December 17, 2010)
Baby Daddy: Joey Aranzeta
Episode 310: June 21, 2010

After her episode aired, Allie left Joey and moved back to New Jersey with baby Aydenn. She no longer speaks to Joey, who has chosen not to be in contact with his son. Allie is currently living with her mother in New Jersey, attending college and working. She started dating a new guy in the summer of 2011, and as of November 2012, the couple is still together. Joey is still living in Texas, attending high school and has a new girlfriend. He will graduate in 2013.

- SEASON FOUR -

LINDSEY HARRISON

Reno, NV
(b. August 17, 1994)

Baby: Aniyah Monroe Harrison-Ponce (b. October 13, 2011)
Baby Daddy: Forest Ponce
Episode 404: April 10, 2012

After she taped her episode, Lindsey claims she caught Forest cheating on her and that when she confronted him, he got physical with her. She told her *Twitter* followers in July 2012 that Forest, who had been using drugs at the time, shoved her to the ground while she was holding their daughter. "Aniyah will not be around drugs and an abusive person," Lindsey told her *Twitter* followers. "My stuff is packed and I'm gone for good. I would never be with a cheater or an abusive man." After the breakup, Lindsey took her daughter and moved to a small town in northern Nevada, where she took a job as a waitress at a restaurant. In October 2012, she moved home to Reno to be closer to her family. She plans to go to the police academy and become a police officer, then attend college and become a detective. She's still pursuing her interest in becoming an MMA cage fighter and is currently in a new relationship.

JORDAN HOWARD

Millersville, PA
(b. November 10, 1993)

Baby: Chase Alexander Zeplin (b. May 31, 2011)
Baby Daddy: Tyler Zeplin
Episode 406: April 24, 2012

A lot has changed for Jordan and her family since the MTV cameras stopped rolling. "My life is a lot better since filming stopped," Jordan says. "Tyler and I moved out and live on our own now." The racial tension between Jordan's mother and Tyler, which Jordan says MTV played up for the cameras, has also completely dissolved. "Tyler and my mom's relationship [is] great!" she says. "[MTV] failed to mention that Tyler and my mom did/do hang out." Jordan and Tyler have also made a lot of progress in their relationship. "We are engaged and plan to be married in 2015," Jordan says. These days, Jordan and Tyler both work at different Pennsylvania grocery stores, and plan to get their son into child modeling.

MYRANDA TREVINO

San Augustine, TX
(b. April 8, 1994)

Baby: Kaylee Michelle Kennemer (b. September 30, 2011)
Baby Daddy: Eric Kennemer
Episode 407: May 1, 2012

When we last saw Myranda, she was having trouble trusting her mother, who struggled with alcoholism and drug addiction, around her daughter Kaylee. She and her baby's father, Eric, moved out of Eric's grandmother's house and into a rundown shack so that they could have their own space. The couple still lives there, but has done extensive work on the house and has even added a bedroom for their daughter. Days before Myranda's episode aired, she and Eric became engaged. The couple is planning to wait a few years before tying the knot, but is currently living together. Myranda chose to go back to high school in the summer of 2012, rather than just obtaining her GED. After graduation, she plans to go to college. Eric currently works and goes to college full-time. Myranda and her mother continue to work on their relationship. Her mother still struggles with dependency issues, but is attempting to get sober.

HOPE HARBERT

Lee's Summit, MO
(b. July 17, 1993)

Baby: Tristan Blaise Lagle (b. August 26, 2011)
Baby Daddy: Ben Lagle
Episode 408: May 8, 2012

After her episode taped, Hope and baby Tristan moved in with Ben, and Hope began attending college in August 2012. "I am going for occupational therapy assistant or physical therapist, haven't decided yet," Hope says. "Although the couple split up for a few months in early 2013, Hope says that they are now doing great. "We are together and he bought me a promise ring," Hope tells us. "He said I can be expecting a proposal soon!"Hope says that her life has definitely changed since she appeared on the show. "We get recognized all the time. People have asked to take pictures with us and have asked for my autograph while I'm working."

SARAH ROBERTS

Chickamauga, GA

Baby: Tinleigh Louise Thomas (b. June 18, 2011)
Baby Daddy: Blake Thomas
Episode 409: May 15, 2012

Three weeks after her daughter, Tinleigh, was born, Sarah's boyfriend, Blake left town. "I felt betrayed, angry and hurt. I'm now a teen mother, and a single mother," Sarah wrote in a guest blog post for *Huff Post Teen*. "I love my daughter more than anything in the world, but the reality is that being a mom at 17 is difficult." Still, Sarah managed to graduate high school with her class and is currently attending college, where she's majoring in psychology. As for Blake, he is currently living across the state line from Sarah in Tennessee. In December 2012, he was arrested in Hamilton County for unlawfully removing a vehicle's registration plate. A month later, he was picked up again by police for driving with a suspended license. In the summer of 2012, Sarah learned that he had impregnated another teenage girl. He is not in Tinleigh's life at all, according to Sarah. "I no longer watch my episode because of Blake," she says, adding that it's unlikely that we will see her on television again. "As far as doing a 'Where Are They Now?' [episode for *16 and Pregnant*] no," Sarah says. "They would want to talk to Blake and about him and I don't want to deal with it. I am and always will be so thankful I wasn't chosen [for *Teen Mom 3*]. The only positive thing of that show is money," she says. "I believe *16 and Pregnant* encourages teen pregnancy. It's no longer realistic."

SABRINA SOLARES

Thompsons Station, TN
(b. April 26, 1994)

Baby: Audrey Animi Williams (b. August 21, 2011)
Baby Daddy: Iman Williams
Episode 410: May 15, 2012

"My life has changed drastically [since filming ended]," Sabrina says. After the reunion show taped, Sabrina and her baby's father, Iman, ended their relationship. "I broke up with Iman due to the fact that he wasn't a great father to Audrey and our relationship was abusive," Sabrina says. After the breakup, Sabrina and her daughter, Audrey, moved back to Los Angeles, where she and Iman are originally from, but she and the baby ended up moving back to Tennessee shortly after to be closer to Sabrina's mother. "Iman has not seen her since then," she says. "I bought him a plane ticket to come see her a long time ago but he still has not come to see her." In August 2012, Sabrina began dating a new guy, and says she's very happy with the way her new boyfriend treats her and Audrey. As of March 2013 she was working at a Walgreens in Tennessee and attending college. She plans to become an elementary school teacher. Iman is currently living near Los Angeles and is about to have another child by his new girlfriend, according to Sabrina.

DEVON BROYLES

Richmond, VA
(b. July 27, 1994)

Baby: Landon Levi Crowder (b. November 4, 2011)
Baby Daddy: Colin Crowder
Episode 411: May 22, 2012

Devon and Colin moved out of Devon's crowded house right after filming their *16 and Pregnant* episode. The couple became engaged in July 2012, but Colin broke up with Devon in February 2013. Both have moved on to new relationships since. Devon obtained her GED and plans to go to college to become a labor and delivery nurse. As of March 2013, she was working part-time at an Italian restaurant. Colin is still in the Army Reserves and works full-time.

KRISTINA ROBINSON

Waskom, TX

Baby: Lukas Todd Hight (b. September 26, 2011)
Baby Daddy: John "Todd" Hight Jr. (d. April 30, 2011)
Episode 412: May 29, 2012

Shortly after her episode aired, Kristina began dating **T.J. Head**, a guy she was friendly with during her pregnancy. After she revealed her new relationship, the mother of Kristina's deceased fiancé hinted on *Facebook* that she held Kristina and her family responsible for her son's death, but later recanted her statements. In April 2012, Kristina married T.J. and, five months later, announced that she was pregnant with her second child. Kristina gave birth to her second son, a boy she named **Tommie**, in January 2013. T.J. has become a father figure to Kristina's other son, **Lukas**.

Chapter 16

87 THINGS YOU MIGHT NOT KNOW ABOUT THE TEEN MOMS

1. **Leah's** twin daughters, **Aliannah** and **Aleeah**, were born on December 16, 2009 – the same day as **Ashley Salazar**'s daughter, **Callie**, and **Lori Wickelhaus**' son, **Aiden**.

2. **Allie Mendoza** fainted during the filming of the season three "Life After Labor" reunion special, causing complete chaos on the set. **Dr. Drew Pinsky** had a crewmember fetch his medical bag from his dressing room and revived her.

3. **Amber** and **Gary** had to receive special permission from Child Protective Services to appear together with their daughter, **Leah**, on the *Teen Mom* season three reunion special.

4. **Leah, Maci**, **Farrah**, **Nikkole Paulun** and **Mackenzie Douthit** were all high school cheerleaders.

5. At least ten of the girls featured on *16 and Pregnant* have gotten pregnant again since their episodes aired. **Jordan Ward**, **Ebony Rendon** and **Brooke Smitherman, Kristina Robinson** and **Leah** all gave birth. **Jenelle** and **Leah** both miscarried. **Markai Durham** and **Jamie McKay** had abortions. At press time, **Danielle Cunningham** and **Nikkole Paulun** were both expecting babies in 2013.

6. **Maci** purposely waited to call producers when she went into labor because she didn't want her son's birth to be filmed. The crew ended up missing **Bentley**'s birth. The rest of the girls from season one all gave birth on-camera.

7. After his marriage to **Leah** fell apart, **Corey Simms** briefly dated **Nikkole**. The two went on a date to a zoo in Columbus, Ohio, with their children in tow, which pissed Leah off.

8. **Leah** and her second husband, **Jeremy Calvert**, spent their honeymoon in the Bahamas, without cameras.

9. Girls appearing on the *Teen Mom* shows receive digital copies of the episodes only hours before they air.

10. Executive Producer **Morgan J. Freeman** was also responsible for the MTV show, *Laguna Beach.*

11. **Maci**'s middle name, Deshane, was also the middle name of her aunt Belinda, who passed away before she was born.

12. **Jenelle**'s sister, **Ashleigh**, was pregnant with triplets in early 2011. She miscarried two of the babies but gave birth to a son in November.

13. **Maci**'s older brother Matt wants nothing to do with MTV and had refused to appear on television. Still, the siblings are very close. In fact, Matt was the first person (other than her boyfriend, **Ryan**) that **Maci** told about her pregnancy.

14. **Chelsea** was shown going into labor at school during her *16 and Pregnant* episode. But she wasn't actually in labor; she just had cramps. Chelsea actually went to the hospital the next day and had her baby.

15. **Dr. Drew Pinsky** once appeared on the game show, *Wheel of Fortune.*

16. **Tyler** used some of his *Teen Mom* money to pay for sister Amber's boob job.

17. The four stars of *Teen Mom 2* all have matching red heart tattoos on their wrists. They got them while in Los Angeles to shoot the season one reunion show in August 2011.

18. Each girl appearing on *16 and Pregnant* is given a Flip video camera. They use it to film the monologue shown at the end of their episode and, in some cases, to capture important events that happen when the MTV film crew is not there. The girls get to keep their camera after they finish filming.

19. **Jo**'s rap name is N.I.C.K. B, which is short for "Nerd In a Cool Kid's Body." He chose to do a rap remix of an **Alicia Keys** love song for his first single in hopes that people would see a more sensitive side of him than they do on *Teen Mom 2*.

20. **Gary** auditioned for the reality weight loss show *The Biggest Loser* in 2009.

21. Although it was never discussed on the show, **Gary Shirley** worked as a nurse's aid for developmentally disabled patients during the filming of the first two seasons of *Teen Mom*.

22. **Kail** and **Jo** conceived their son, Isaac, on prom night. Leah and Corey also conceived their twins on prom night.

23. **Leah** took five pregnancy tests when she suspected that she was expecting. Even though all of them came back positive, she made her mother take her to the hospital to find out for sure.

24. **Gary** was bullied as a child over his weight.

25. **Farrah**, **Amber**, **Maci** and **Catelynn**, snuck into the taping of the *16 and Pregnant* season 3 "Life After Labor" reunion special. They watched the show from the audience and later went backstage to meet the new crop of girls.

26. **Amber** and **Gary** originally planned to name their daughter Madison.

27. **Kail** has said that when she is in a store and sees any of her *Teen Mom* co-stars on the cover of a tabloid magazine, she will turn the magazine over.

28. The youngest girl to ever be featured on *16 and Pregnant* was **Taylor Lumas** of season three. She was 15.

29. When **Mackenzie Douthit** first told her boyfriend, **Josh**, that she was pregnant he didn't believe her. In fact, he made her take a pregnancy test in front of him to prove it. Afterwards, he took a pregnancy test himself to see if the tests worked. (Just for the record, Josh wasn't pregnant.)

30. **Amber**'s episode of *16 and Pregnant* was the show's "pilot." It was shown to the network to see if MTV wanted to pick up the show.

31. **Christinna Robinson** of *16 and Pregnant* season two threatened to not complete the voiceovers for her episode unless producers edited out a few conversations she had with her boyfriend's grandmother in which they discussed her promiscuity.

32. **Kail** named her son **Isaac** after **Isaac Hanson** of the 1990s band Hanson.

33. **Jenelle** once tried to use a tabloid magazine with her name and picture on the cover as proof of ID when she was buying cigarettes.

34. **Amber** was not allowed to attend the *Teen Mom* season four reunion special in New York City because she was on probation at the time for a recent drug arrest and the judge handling her case would not allow it, although MTV did try.

35. **Maci** did not tell her then-boyfriend, **Ryan**, that she had sent in an audition tape to be on *16 and Pregnant*.

36. The clothing company Aeropostale contacted MTV in the summer of 2011 to request that none of the *Teen Mom* stars be allowed to wear their clothing on the show. **Gary**, who frequently sported the company's T-shirts during filming, continued to wear Aeropostale apparel while filming the show, but the company's logo had to be blurred.

37. Although she lived very close to *16 and Pregnant* season 4 star **Alex Sekella** (and they shared mutual friends), producers asked **Kail** to avoid associating with her.

38. The only girl from the *Teen Mom* and *Teen Mom 2* series that does not have a tattoo is **Farrah**.

39. Dr. Drew made every single girl from season 3 cry at least once during the "Life After Labor" reunion special.

40. **Jenelle's** father **Robert**, who lives in Pennsylvania, had no idea his daughter had ended up pregnant and on a television show,

until reporters from *Star* magazine called him and members of his family, looking for an interview.

41. **Kail** once bailed **Jenelle** out of jail.

42. **Kieffer** is of Jamaican and Irish decent.

43. **Ryan** rarely, if ever, watched an episode of *Teen Mom* because he didn't like how MTV portrayed him or his family.

44. **Leah** has a younger brother named Ezekiel Isaac that is not shown on *Teen Mom 2*.

45. MTV employees monitor every cast member's social network postings. Before *Teen Mom 2* aired in 2011, all of the girls were required to disable their Formspring accounts.

46. The girls are contractually required to participate in the "Life After Labor" reunion special with Dr. Drew. MTV pays for their travel accommodations.

47. Maci says that she knew she had to end things with Ryan after she watched the first season of *Teen Mom* on TV and saw how poorly he treated her.

48. **Farrah**'s autobiography, *My Teenage Dream Ended*, peaked at #11 on the New York Times' E-books Best Sellers List.

49. The "No Easy Decision" special in which **Markai Durham** discussed her abortion was considered so controversial; MTV scheduled it to air at 11:30 PM with no commercials.

50. The couple that adopted **Lori Wickelhaus**' son did not allow their name to appear in the episode, or any of the press that followed the airing of her episode.

51. **Maci**'s natural hair color is strawberry blond.

52. In February 2012, **Catelynn** acted as a labor coach for a woman who was placing her son for adoption with the same parents that adopted Catelynn and **Tyler**'s daughter, **Carly**. Catelynn watched as Carly's adopted little brother was born.

53. Everyone that speaks on camera during the filming of these shows has to have a microphone on — even the babies!

54. Had her son been a girl, **Kail** has said that she and **Jo** would have named her Brooklyn Brielle Shaunice.

55. **Maci** doesn't allow fans to take photos with Bentley.

56. MTV will not allow anyone that appears to be over the age of 30 to sit in the audience of its reunion show tapings for *16 and Pregnant* or the *Teen Mom* shows.

57. Although many of the cast members of *Teen Mom* and *Teen Mom 2* smoke cigarettes, they are never shown on camera smoking. MTV also edits out any underage drinking and drug use.

58. **Chelsea** is friends with **Britney Spears**' sister, **Jamie Lynn**. In February 2012, they took a trip to New Orleans together, along with Daniel Payne, star of MTV's *Caged*.

59. In March 2013, *16 and Pregnant* season 4 star **Danielle Cunningham** revealed that she had been addicted to heroin during the months before she became pregnant with her second child.

60. **Amber** suffered from gestational diabetes during her pregnancy.

61. **Chelsea**'s father, **Randy**, is often seen on *Teen Mom 2*, but her stepmother, **Rita**, has never appeared on the show. She also decided against appearing on Chelsea's *16 and Pregnant* episode, and *Teen Mom 2* because she did not like the show.

62. **Kail** and **Jenelle** are both atheists. "Being ignorant is pushing your beliefs on other people," Kail vented on *Twitter*. "I can still be a good person if I don't believe in God."

63. *Teen Mom 3* cast member **Katie Yeager** met her baby's father, **Joey**, after their parents started dating.

64. **Maci** and **Ryan** considered the name Ryder before deciding on the name Bentley. They planned to name their child Bentley whether it was a boy or a girl.

65. **Morgan J. Freeman** met a woman named Katie at the hospital the day **Maci** gave birth to **Bentley**. The couple eventually ended up getting married in October 2012, and invited Maci to their wedding.

66. **Maci** accidentally hit a parked car while filming a scene for *Teen Mom* at Chattanooga State University in October 2010. Maci and her camera crew left without reporting the accident, essentially

committing a hit-and-run. The incident was filmed by onlookers, and the driver eventually filed a police report against Maci.

67. Shortly after appearing on the fourth season of *16 and Pregnant*, Sarah Roberts' baby-daddy, **Blake**, impregnated another teenage girl.

68. The girls' middle names are as follows: **Chelsea Anne**; **Leah Dawn**; **Jenelle Lauren**; **Kailyn Rae**; **Catelynn Judith**; **Maci Deshane**; **Farrah Lynn**; **Amber LeAnn**.

69. Growing up, **Kail**'s mother gave her the nickname "chunky monkey," which she hated.

70. In September 2011, **Gary** got **Amber**'s name tattooed on his back. Four months later, after the couple broke up (again) he had the giant tattoo covered up.

71. **Jenelle** graduated high school a semester early.

72. MTV did not tell the season four girls who had been chosen for *Teen Mom 3*. Instead, the girls had to find out online and from each other who had been picked.

73. **Amber**, her daughter, **Leah**, and her mother, Tonya, all share the middle name: Leann.

74. Both **Maci** and *Teen Mom 3*'s **Katie Yeager** competed in beauty pageants as children.

75. The girls do their own hair and makeup for the show, with the exception of the reunion specials, in which MTV provides hair and makeup artists to help them.

76. **Leah** and **Jeremy** bought their wedding bands at a pawn shop.

77. **Kail** and her husband **Javi** have matching infinity sign tattoos.

78. One of the only places the cameras are not allowed to follow the girls is the bathroom. If the girl goes into the bathroom and closes the door, the camera crew is not allowed to open the door and go in.

79. **Farrah** disliked the name that her sister **Ashley** had picked out for her first child. Right before Ashley gave birth, Farrah urged her sister to change the name to Sayechelle, Serrica or Sapphire.

80. **Christinna Robinson** was the only girl that did not allow MTV to come back and film a segment for the "Where Are They Now?" episode.

81. **Chelsea** celebrated her 21st birthday at Rain nightclub at the Palms Hotel in Las Vegas – the same club that the original cast of *The Real World: Las Vegas* worked at.

82. **Farrah** invited a paparazzi crew from Splash News into the operating room with her to capture her nose job and chin implant surgery in October 2012.

83. In January 2012, **Maci** and her then-boyfriend **Kyle King** were kicked out of an Anaheim, California hotel for physically fighting.

The couple – and several of Maci's friends – were escorted off hotel property after the incident.

84. **Maci** has never publically admitted to getting a boob job.

85. **Corey Simms** proposed to his fiancé, **Miranda Patterson** in November 2012 by hanging an engagement ornament on the Christmas tree. This is the same way **Leah**'s second husband **Jeremy Calvert** proposed in December 2011.

86. In February 2012, **Jo Rivera** did a radio interview and was asked which of **Kail**'s fellow *Teen Mom 2* co-stars he'd hook up with if he had to choose. Reluctantly, he chose **Chelsea**.

87. **Leah** and **Corey** got in trouble with producers for posting their wedding photos on Leah's *Facebook* fan page, before their wedding episode aired.

Chapter 17

TEEN MOM SURVIVAL GUIDE – A TO Z

ABORTION: On December 28, 2010, MTV aired a special called "No Easy Decision" in which **Markai Durham** discussed why she chose to end her second pregnancy.

ADAM LIND: Chelsea's baby daddy and father of **Aubree**.

ADOPTION: Three girls – **Catelynn, Lori Wickelhaus** and **Ashley Salazar** – chose to give their babies up. The aftermath of Catelynn's decision is a key plotline in the *Teen Mom* series.

ALGONAC (MI): Hometown of **Catelynn** and **Tyler**. Pop: 4,110.

ALEEAH & ALIANNAH SIMMS: Twin daughters of **Leah** and **Corey**. Born on December 16, 2009.

ALETHEA MONTANTE: Former neighbor and close friend of **Farrah**. Featured on fourth season of *Teen Mom*.

ALLENTOWN (PA): Hometown of **Kail** and **Alexandria Sekella**. Inspiration for 1980s hit by **Billy Joel**. Birthplace of actress **Amanda Seyfried**. 12th most conservative city in America.

ANDERSON (IN): Hometown of **Amber** and **Gary**. Pop: 56,129. Median income: $32, 577. Birthplace of the postage stamp vending machine.

ANOREXIA: Eating disorder that afflicted **Kayla Jackson** (*16 and Pregnant*, season three) throughout her entire pregnancy. When Kayla nearly passed out one day, it is discovered that she hadn't eaten, in hopes that she would stop gaining weight.

APRIL BALTIERRA: Catelynn's mom. She became the stepmother of Catelynn's boyfriend **Tyler** when she married his father, **Butch**.

ASHLEY DANIELSON: Farrah's sister. She appeared on Farrah's *16 and Pregnant* episode, as well as throughout the *Teen Mom* series.

ARABELLA SEKELLA-McCANN: Daughter of **Alexandria Sekella** and **Matt McCann.** Featured on *Teen Mom 3*. Born on July 18, 2011.

ASHLEIGH EVANS: Jenelle's sister. Ashleigh appeared on a few episodes of *Teen Mom*. In 2012, she got into a bitter feud with Jenelle after she claimed that Jenelle stole money from her.

AUBREE HOUSKA: The daughter of **Chelsea Houska** and **Adam Lind**. Born on September 7, 2009.

- B-

BARBARA EVANS: Jenelle's mom. The pair often clash about Jenelle's partying, boyfriends, and how Jenelle's son, **Jace**, should be raised. Jenelle signed over parental rights to Barbara during the filming of *Teen Mom 2*.

BENTLEY EDWARDS: Maci and **Ryan**'s son. His appearance on the show caused the name Bentley to become the fastest growing boy's name of 2011, according to the Social Security Administration.

BETHANY CHRISTIAN SERVICES: Michigan adoption agency that **Catelynn** and **Tyler** used to find their daughter's adoptive parents.

BITTERSWEET BLESSINGS: The autobiography released in 2012 by season two cast member **Ashley Salazar**.

BOOB JOBS: Jenelle, **Maci** and **Farrah** all had breast augmentation surgery since the birth of their children.

BRANDON & TERESA DAVIS: The adoptive parents of **Catelynn** and **Tyler**'s daughter, **Carly**. They appear in several episodes of *Teen Mom*.

BRITTANY TRUETT: Jenelle was videotaped beating up her former friend in March 2011. When the footage went viral, both were arrested along with another girl.

BUTCH BALTIERRA: Tyler's dad and **Catelynn**'s stepdad. His fondness for breaking the law and illegal drugs often landed him in the slammer throughout the series. His alleged attack on Catelynn's mother served as major storyline of the show's fourth season.

- C -

CARLY ELIZABETH DAVIS: Catelynn and **Tyler's** daughter (b. May 18, 2009). She was adopted at birth by **Brandon and Teresa Davis**.

CHARLES ANDREW LEWIS: Father of **Jenelle Evans**' son, **Jace**. Though he is referenced on *Teen Mom 2*, he never appeared on the show.

CHATTANOOGA (TN): Maci's hometown. Pop. 167,674. Birthplace of the tow truck.

COUNCIL BLUFFS (IA): Hometown of **Farrah Abraham**. Birth place of inventor Lee De Forest, known as the "Grandfather of Television."

COREY SIMMS: The father of **Leah**'s twin daughters. They married on October 17, 2010. The wedding served as part of the first season finale of *Teen Mom 2*. Corey and Leah's divorce was finalized on June 21, 2011.

CUSTODY: One of the most hotly contested issues on the show. **Amber** and **Gary**, **Maci** and **Ryan**, **Kail** and **Jo**, and **Jenelle** and her mother, **Barbara** often got into arguments over how much time they got to spend with their children.

- D -

DALIS CONNELL: Former girlfriend of **Ryan Edwards**. Appeared on the fourth season of *Teen Mom*.

DANIEL ALVAREZ: Briefly dated **Farrah** during the summer of 2011. Their courtship was filmed and shown during the fourth season of *Teen Mom*.

DAWN BAKER: The adoption counselor who helped **Catelynn** and **Tyler** find adoptive parents for their daughter **Carly**. Dawn was also instrumental in getting Catelynn cast on *16 and Pregnant*.

DAWN SPEARS: Mother of **Leah Messer** (and a former teen mom herself).

DEBRA DANIELSON: Farrah's mother. She is arrested during the first season of *Teen Mom* for assaulting her daughter.

DEREK UNDERWOOD: Farrah's ex-boyfriend and the father of her daughter, **Sophia**. He was killed in a car accident on December 28, 2008 at the age of 18.

DEVOIN AUSTIN II: Absentee father of *Teen Mom 3* star **Briana DeJesus**' daughter, **Nova**.

DIA SOKOL SAVAGE: Creator of *16 and Pregnant* and *Teen Mom*. She has also written and produced several independent films.

DR. DREW PINSKY: Host of the "Life After Labor" finale specials, as well as the season finales reunions. In 2011, he revealed that several of the *Teen Mom* girls often call him to chat and get advice.

DRUGS: In her memoir, **Farrah** reveals that she used drugs, particularly cocaine, before and after her daughter **Sophia** was born. **Butch**, **Jenelle**, **Ebony Jackson** and **Jo Rivera** have all been arrested for drug-related offenses.

DUSTIN SULLIVAN: **Jenelle**'s court appointed attorney. He had no idea that his client was an MTV celebrity when they first met.

- E -

ENGAGEMENTS: Several of the girls became engaged during their time on MTV. Cameras rolled as **Leah** accepted a proposal from Corey during the first season of *Teen Mom 2*. While filming the third season of the show, Jenelle accepted a proposal from **Gary Head**. (The couple split soon after). During the fourth season of *Teen Mom 2*, Kail gets engaged to boyfriend **Javi Marroquin**.

- F -

FACEBOOK FAN PAGES: Most of the girls featured on *16 and Pregnant* and the *Teen Mom* shows have their own *Facebook* fan page, some of which are run by the girls themselves. Although they were forbidden by MTV to do so, several of the girls from the third season of *16 and Pregnant* used these fan pages to campaign for a spot on *Teen Mom 3*.

FLORIDA: The summer home of Farrah and daughter, Sophia, in 2011.

- G -

GED: **Chelsea** finally obtained her GED in 2012, after struggling for years to get it. **Amber** is using her time in prison to work towards hers.

GRADUATION: Several of the girls, including **Maci** and **Kail**, graduated from high school early after finding out that they were pregnant.

GARY HEAD: Jenelle became engaged to the Marine in May 2012, after dating him for a few months. The relationship ended after both were arrested after a fight in June 2012, in which Jenelle claimed Gary beat her up and tried to strangle her with a bed sheet.

GARY SHIRLEY: Father of **Amber**'s daughter, **Leah**. Gary was awarded full custody in December 2011.

- H -

HONESDALE (PA): Kail's hometown. This tiny Pennsylvania town, located 32 miles northeast of Scranton, has a population of about 5,000.

- I -

ISAAC ELLIOTT RIVERA: Kail and **Jo**'s son. Born on January 18, 2010.

- J -

JACE VAHN EVANS: Jenelle's son. Born on August 9, 2009. Before he was a year old, Jenelle signed over custody of him to her mother, Barbara. Jace's father is **Charles Andrew Lewis**.

JAMES DUFFY: Jenelle's boss during the third season of *Teen Mom 2*. Their relationship soured and Jenelle had James arrested for cyber-stalking after he posted photos of her partying on his *Twitter* account.

JAMIE McKAY: Featured on the third season of *16 and Pregnant*, Jamie shocked her Twitter followers in October 2012 when she revealed she had recently had an abortion.

JEREMY CALVERT: Leah's second husband. They started dating in August 2011. Jeremy proposed on Christmas and the couple married in April 2012.

JO RIVERA: Kail's ex-fiancé and the father of her son, **Isaac**. The couple struggled to co-parent after their breakup and often fought about the way their son should be raised.

JORDAN WARD-FINDER: Jordan was already pregnant for the second time when she filmed the *16 and Pregnant* season 3 "Life After

Labor" reunion special, causing one MTV production member to call her "an embarrassment" to the show.

JORDAN WENNER: Kail's ex-boyfriend. Jordan began dating Kail during the second season of *Teen Mom 2*. Their relationship ended in the spring of 2011.

JOSE "JAVI" MARROQUIN: Married Kail in a secret ceremony in Allentown, Pennsylvania in September 2012. The ceremony took place nearly one year to the day that they made their relationship official.

- K -

KATIE YEAGER: The Wyoming teen appeared on season four of *16 and Pregnant* and was later chosen to appear on *Teen Mom 3*.

KIEFFER DELP: Jenelle's on-off boyfriend has a long history of run-ins with the law. Both were arrested together multiple times, starting in October 2010.

KYLE KING: Maci's boyfriend during the second, third and fourth seasons of *Teen Mom*. They moved in together and were considering marriage before breaking up in January 2012. The couple briefly reunited during the summer of 2012, but ended things for good that September.

KYLE REGAL: Maci briefly dated the Supercross racer after breaking up with Kyle King. Although he was never seen on the show, Maci was dating him when she filmed the *Teen Mom* season four reunion special. They broke up in May 2012.

- L -

LAUREN DOLGEN: MTV development executive who came up with the idea for *16 and Pregnant* in 2008. She later served as an executive producer for its spin-offs, *Teen Mom* and *Teen Mom 2*.

LEAH LEANN SHIRLEY: Amber and Gary's daughter. Leah was born on November 12, 2008.

LIFE AFTER LABOR: The "Life After Labor" reunion specials are filmed at the end of each season of *16 and Pregnant*. The girls are contractually obligated to participate in the shows, which take place in either Los Angeles or New York City.

MACKENZIE DOUTHIT: One of four girls chosen for *Teen Mom 3*, she was also featured on the fourth season of *16 and Pregnant*.

MEGAN NELSON: **Chelsea**'s best friend and former roommate. Megan moved out of the house she shared with Chelsea after Adam moved in. In July 2011, Megan became a teen mom herself when she gave birth to her son Hunter at the age of 19.

MICHAEL ABRAHAM: **Farrah**'s dad. Michael was constantly screamed at and belittled by his daughter during the filming of *Teen Mom*. Michael is now officially divorced from Farrah's mother, Debra, and lives in Austin, Texas.

MILITARY: Several of the fathers featured on *16 and Pregnant* have gone on to serve, including **Josh Rendon** (husband of **Ebony Jackson**), and **Brian Finder** (husband of **Jordan Ward**).

MORGAN J. FREEMAN: The executive producer of *16 and Pregnant*, *Teen Mom* and *Teen Mom 2*. He also produced other shows for MTV including *Laguna Beach* and *Maui Fever*.

MY TEENAGE DREAM ENDED: Farrah's 2012 memoir made the *New York Times*' E-book Best Sellers list, while the accompanying music CD was overwhelmingly panned by critics for its heavy use of auto-tune and rambling lyrics.

- N -

NAZARETH (PA): The Pennsylvania town that **Kail** was living in when she filmed her episode of *16 and Pregnant*.

NASHVILLE (TN): The hometown of **Kyle King**. **Maci** moved here during the second season of *Teen Mom* to be closer to her boyfriend.

- O -

OAK ISLAND (NC): The small seaside town in North Carolina that **Jenelle** and her mother, **Barbara**, call home. Pop: 6,571.

- P -

PUBLIC SPEAKING: Several of the *Teen Mom* girls – including **Catelynn** and **Maci** – have spoken at high schools and colleges about preventing teen pregnancy. Catelynn and **Tyler** also speak as adoption advocates.

- Q -

QUESTIONNAIRES: The girls being considered for *16 and Pregnant* have to fill out a series of questionnaires and complete a psychology test before being cast for the show.

- R -

RANDY HOUSKA: Chelsea's dad. Randy has been outspoken about his hatred for her on-and-off-again boyfriend, Adam Lind.

REHAB: In the spring of 2011, Amber Portwood and Jenelle Evans both spent time in the same drug rehab facility in Malibu, California, with Amber checking in just after Jenelle left. In March 2013, MTV once again paid for Jenelle to attend a rehab facility to help her battle her addition to various drugs.

ROBBIE KIDD: Robbie dated Leah Messer for three years in high school. The couple broke up right before Leah met Corey. Leah briefly dated Robbie again in 2010 after splitting with Corey. During season two of *Teen Mom 2*, Leah admits that she cheated with Robbie just days before she married Corey in October 2010.

ROCKVILLE CORRECTIONAL FACILITY: Amber Portwood was sentenced to five years at this women's prison in Indiana after quitting drug court in June 2012. In October 2012, MTV sent Dr. Drew Pinsky into the prison to film the *Amber Behind Bars* special.

RYAN EDWARDS: The former fiancé of Maci Bookout and the father of her son, Bentley. After Ryan and Maci split during season one of *Teen Mom*, they constantly battled over custody of their son.

- S -

SCRANTON (PA): Jenelle's birthplace. Home of the fictional Dunder Mifflin paper company.

SHAWN PORTWOOD: Amber's older brother. Shawn was featured on several episodes of *Teen Mom*, and often spoke for Amber in the press.

He has been outspoken about his dislike of MTV and the *Teen Mom* brand.

SOFTBALL: Both Maci and Chelsea played in high school.

SOPHIA LAURENT ABRAHAM: Farrah's daughter was born on February 23, 2009, two months after her father, Derek, died in a car accident.

STORMIE CLARK: The mother of Farrah Abraham's baby-daddy, Derek Underwood, and grandmother of Sophia. She has tried unsuccessfully to establish a relationship with her granddaughter since Sophia's birth.

SUBOXONE: A drug used to treat opiate addiction to which Amber was addicted to before going to prison.

SUICIDE: In June 2011, Amber attempted suicide at her home in Anderson, Indiana. She was transported to a local hospital after her boyfriend at the time, Gary Shirley, called 9-1-1 after being alarmed about her behavior.

- T -

TATTOOS: Nearly all of the *Teen Mom* and *Teen Mom 2* girls are fond of getting tattoos. Several of the girls have gotten tattoos in honor of their children.

TORI RHYNE: The on-and-off-again best friend of Jenelle Evans since middle school, Tori has appeared on many episodes of *Teen Mom 2*, as well as Jenelle's *16 and Pregnant* episode. During season two, Jenelle and Tori got into a physical fight on camera.

TWINS: Two girls featured on *16 and Pregnant* have had twins: **Leah** and **Jennifer Del Rio**.

TWITTER: Maci has the most followers – over one million!

TYLER BALTIERRA: **Catelynn**'s fiancé and **Carly**'s birth father. Tyler and Catelynn have been together since 7th grade and plan to marry in July 2013.

- U -

UNPLANNED PREGNANCIES: None of the pregnancies featured on *16 and Pregnant* were planned, however, it has been rumored that there have been girls that have gotten pregnant on purpose in hopes of making it on the show.

- V -

VEE TORRES: **Jo Rivera** girlfriend during the third and fourth seasons of *Teen Mom 2*. Kail does not get along with Vee, which causes major problems between her and Jo.

VIACOM: Parent company of MTV. The cast members receive their checks from the company.

VOICEOVERS: The girls are required to read the scripts written for them by MTV writers. The voiceovers are usually recorded in recording studios in the girls' hometowns. The girls from the *Teen Mom* shows usually record their voiceovers in New York City.

- W -

WALMART: The favorite hangout of many of the girls featured on the shows and former place of employment of Jenelle Evans' mother, Barbara. It is also the store that Gary purchased a $26.98 engagement ring for Amber.

WEDDINGS: Several weddings have been filmed for *Teen Mom 2*, including Corey and Leah's wedding in October 2010, Leah's wedding to Jeremy in April 2012 and Kail's wedding to Javi Marroquin in September 2012.

WEST VIRGINIA: Home state of Leah and Corey. Leah has lived in various towns across the state, including Elkview, Charleston and Clendenin.

- X -

X-RATED PHOTOS: In May 2012, Kieffer sold scandalous, topless photos of Jenelle to a tabloid. Four months later, **James Duffy**, her former boss and boyfriend, posted sexual photos of Jenelle on Twitter.

- Y -

YEAR ROUND BROWN: The tanning salon in Sioux Falls, South Dakota, that Chelsea started working at during the second season of *Teen Mom 2*. She quit in 2012.

- Z -

ZERO: The number of dollars most family members and friends of the girls on *16 and Pregnant* earn for appearing on the show.

Photo Credits:

Page 5: Splash News Service
Page 6: Jason Winslow / Splash News
Page 7: Jackson Lee / Splash News
Page 9: Splash News / Kail Lowry
Page 10: Jackson Lee / Splash
Page 15: Jen Lowery / Splash
Page 23: Splash News
Page 30: Splash News
Page 36: Courtesy / Jamie McKay
Page 40: Courtesy / Danielle Cunningham
Page 42: Splash News
Page 44: Splash News
Page 48: Splash News
Page 53: Splash News
Page 54: Splash News
Page 56: Splash News
Page 59: Splash News
Page 61: Courtesy / Daniel Alvarez
Page 62: Courtesy / Daniel Alvarez
Page 65: Splash / Alethea Montante
Page 67: Courtesy / Stormie Clark
Page 70: Courtesy / Stormie Clark
Page 75: Courtesy / Stormie Clark
Page 85: Courtesy / Kail Lowry
Page 86: Courtesy / Kail Lowry
Page 98: Splash News
Page 99: Splash News
Page 101: Law enforcement photo
Page 102: Law enforcement photo
Page 103: Law enforcement photo
Page 104: Law enforcement photo
Page 105: Law enforcement photo
Page 106: Sulia.com
Page 112: Splash News
Page 115: Splash News
Page 115: Courtesy / Amy Nichols
Page 122: Splash News
Page 125: Splash News
Page 127: Law enforcement photo
Page 131: Law enforcement photo
Page 133: Law enforcement photo
Page 134: Law enforcement photo
Page 135: Courtesy / Danielle Cunningham
Page 138: Law enforcement photo
Page 141: Twitter.com
Page 153: Law enforcement photo
Page 157: Splash News
Page 159: Courtesy Lopatcong P.D.
Page 161: Law enforcement photo
Page 166: Courtesy / Butch Baltierra
Page 173: Facebook
Page 183: Courtesy / Ebony Jackson
Page 184: Courtesy / Ebony Jackson
Page 186: Courtesy / Ebony Jackson
Page 188: Courtesy / Jamie McKay
Page 190: Courtesy / Nicole Fokos
Page 214: Ashley Majeski

Made in the USA
Columbia, SC
29 January 2021

31949909R00137